LARSON, BOSWELL, KANOLD, STIFF

Passport
to Mathematics

BOOK 1

An ... ers

Answe... ...n lesson to check
homev... ...cher's Edition and
the Co...

W9-CND-027

McDougal Littell
A HOUGHTON MIFFLIN COMPANY
Evanston, Illinois • Boston • Dallas

ISBN: 0-395-89635-5

 23456789-BEI-02 01 00 99 98

Answers for Lesson 1.1, pages 5–7

Ongoing Assessment

1. Beginning with B, choose every third letter. Next three letters are N, Q, T.

2. Choose the first letter after the previous letter, choose the second letter, choose the third letter, choose the fourth letter, and so on. Next three letters are K, P, V.

Practice and Problem Solving

1. Each number increases by 8.

2. 56, 64, and 72

3. No; yes; only 104 is divisible by 8.

4. Answers vary.

5. Each number is two more than the previous number. 9, 11, 13

6. Each number is five less than the previous number. 30, 25, 20

7. Each number is three times the previous number. 405, 1215, 3645

8. Each number is three more than the previous number. 15, 18, 21

9. Each denominator is twice the previous one. $\frac{1}{32}$, $\frac{1}{64}$, $\frac{1}{128}$

10. Each denominator is one more than the previous one. $\frac{1}{5}$, $\frac{1}{6}$, $\frac{1}{7}$

11. Starting with A, list every third letter. M, P, S

12. Alternate a forward listing of the alphabet with a backward listing of the alphabet. C, X, D

13. Starting at Z, working backward, list every other letter of the alphabet. R, P, N

14. The 1st, 3rd, 5th, . . . terms in the pattern are the letters of the alphabet starting with A. The 2nd, 4th, 6th, . . . terms in the pattern are the letters of the alphabet starting at N. C, P, D

15.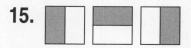

(continued)

16.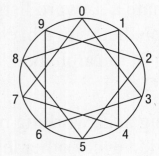

17. 8, 16, 32, 64, 128; the sum of each row is twice the sum of the previous row.

18. Week 12

19. A pattern for the products is as follows:

Count up to middle number

$$1111 \times 1111 \quad = \quad 1234321$$

Middle number is number of digits in original number

Count down from middle number

20. a.

The next seven multiples are 15, 18, 21, 24, 27, 30, and 33. If you find more multiples, the design is retraced.

(continued)

Answers for Lesson 1.1, pages 5–7 (cont.)

20. b.

4 as a factor

5 as a factor

6 as a factor

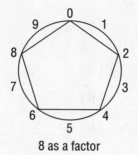
7 as a factor

8 as a factor

The circle designs for the multiples of 4 and 6 are the same; The designs for multiples of 3 and 7 are the same.

c. 43: repeats the pattern of multiples of 3 or 7 to form a 10-pointed star; 65: repeats the pattern of multiples of 5 to form a straight line between 0 and 5. Last digit determines design.

21. C

22. D

23. Answers vary.

Answers for Lesson 1.2, pages 9–11

Ongoing Assessment

1. Soccer; answers vary.

2. Answers vary.

Practice and Problem Solving

1.

	Parker	Whittier	Madison
Bicycle	$89.00	$99.00	$84.00
Movie ticket	$5.50	$7.00	$4.75
Rollerblades	$48.50	$54.00	$47.25

2. The costs of the items in Whittier are the greatest and the costs of the items in Madison are the least.

3. The greatest wages occur in the town with the greatest costs. The lowest wages occur in the town with the lowest costs.

4. a. Sneakers; sneakers
   b. 35–44

5. a. Limes and oranges
   b. 1995

6.   Schools Owning a CD-ROM Computer

	Elementary	Middle	High
1993	4457	2326	4168
1994	11,794	4874	7724
1995	16,816	6170	9063

7. Elementary schools

8. 1994

9. *Sample answer:* the number of CD-ROM computers increased each year for all schools.

10. D

11. Answers vary.

Answers for Lesson 1.3, pages 13–15

Ongoing Assessment

1. and 2.

1 ② 3 ④ 5 ⑥ 7 ⑧ 9 ⑩ 11 ⑫

13 ⑭ 15 ⑯ 17 ⑱ 19 ⑳ 21 ㉒ 23 ㉔

25 ㉖ 27 ㉘ 29 ㉚ 31 ㉜ 33 ㉞ 35 �36

3. They are multiples of 6.

Practice and Problem Solving

1. 1 2 3 4 ⑤ 6 7 8 9 ⑩

11 12 13 14 ⑮ 16 17 18 19 ⑳

21 22 23 24 ㉕ 26 27 28 29 ㉚

31 32 33 34 ㉟ 36 37 38 39 ㊵

41 42 43 44 ㊺ 46 47 48 49 ㊿

They are multiples of 10.

2.
SART	TARS	ARST	RAST ; 24
SATR	TASR	ARTS	RATS
SRAT	TRAS	ASRT	RSAT
SRTA	TRSA	ASTR	RSTA
STAR	TSAR	ATRS	RTAS
STRA	TSRA	ATSR	RTSA

3.
Shorts, blue shirt	Jeans, blue shirt	Sweatpants, blue shirt
Shorts, white shirt	Jeans, white shirt	Sweatpants, white shirt
Shorts, knit shirt	Jeans, knit shirt	Sweatpants, knit shirt

(continued)

Answers for Lesson 1.3, pages 13–15 (cont.)

4. 27

Shorts, white shirt, sandals
Shorts, white shirt, sneakers
Shorts, white shirt, casual
Shorts, blue shirt, sandals
Shorts, blue shirt, sneakers
Shorts, blue shirt, casual
Shorts, knit shirt, sandals
Shorts, knit shirt, sneakers
Shorts, knit shirt, casual

Jeans, white shirt, sandals
Jeans, white shirt, sneakers
Jeans, white shirt, casual
Jeans, blue shirt, sandals
Jeans, blue shirt, sneakers
Jeans, blue shirt, casual
Jeans, knit shirt, sandals
Jeans, knit shirt, sneakers
Jeans, knit shirt, casual

Sweatpants, white shirt, sandals
Sweatpants, white shirt, sneakers
Sweatpants, white shirt, casual
Sweatpants, blue shirt, sandals
Sweatpants, blue shirt, sneakers
Sweatpants, blue shirt, casual
Sweatpants, knit shirt, sandals
Sweatpants, knit shirt, sneakers
Sweatpants, knit shirt, casual

5. Even; $2 + 4$, $6 + 8$

6. Even; $1 + 3$, $5 + 7$

7. Odd; $2 + 1$, $4 + 3$

8. 24, 60

9. 30, 60; yes; no; yes

10. Yes

11. 6, 7, 8, 9, 10, 11, 12

12. 18

13. 684

14. 4640

15. 24;

1359	3159	5139	9135
1395	3195	5193	9153
1539	3519	5319	9315
1593	3591	5391	9351
1935	3915	5913	9513
1953	3951	5931	9531

(continued)

16. a. $.65;

Quarters	Dimes	Nickels
2	1	1
2		3
1	4	
1	3	2
1	2	4
1	1	6
1		8
	6	1
	5	3
	4	5
	3	7
	2	9
	1	11
		13

b. 2 quarters, 1 dime, and 1 nickel uses only 4 coins. 13 nickels uses 13 coins.

17. C

18. Answers vary.

Answers for Lesson 1.4, pages 17–20

Ongoing Assessment

1. Answers vary.

2. *Sample answer:* gas is cheaper, shorter distances to drive.

Practice and Problem Solving

1. *Sample answer:* percent of involvement in sports

2. *Sample answer:* population density

3. About 44

4. About 56

5. **a.** Hiking

   b. Camping, hiking, skiing, sailing

6. **a.** Pennsylvania

   b. Texas

7. **a.** Never; it is the largest section of the circle.

   b. Yes; the sections are about the same size.

8.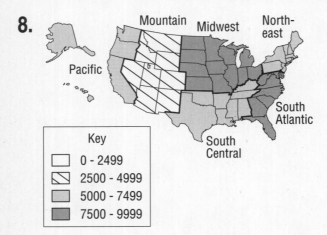

9. *Sample answer:*
   1997: About 75
   1998: About 190
   1999: About 240
   2000: About 420
   2001: About 520
   The graph may show the projected number of households, out of 1000, that are connected to the internet.

10. 252,890; table

11. Less; graph

12. C

13. D

14. Answers vary.

Answers for Spiral Review, page 20

1. 7×9
2. 2×8
3. 4×9
4. 3×17
5. 8×7
6. 27×3
7. 5×15
8. 21×3
9. Yes

10. No
11. Yes
12. No
13. No, too long
14. Yes, possible
15. Yes, possible
16. No, too small
17. $108

Answers for Mid-Chapter Assessment, page 21

1. B
2. A
3. C
4. 6 weeks
5. Bread, eggs, oranges

6. Bread: 1995
   Eggs: 1995
   Chicken: 1993
   Oranges: 1995
7. 32
8. Tell problems
9. Similar; factors are ranked in the same order.
10. 32

Answers for Lesson 1.5, pages 23–25

Ongoing Assessment

1. 8   **2.** Answers vary.

Practice and Problem Solving

1.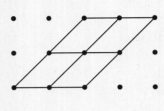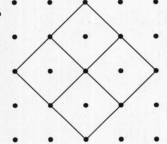

2.

3.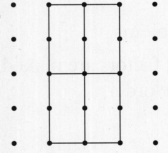

4.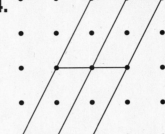

5. *Sample answer:*

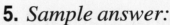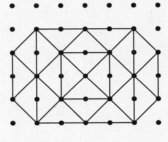

6. *Sample answer:*

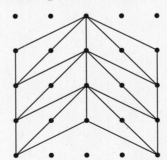

(continued)

Answers for Lesson 1.5, pages 23–25 (cont.)

7. *Sample answer:*

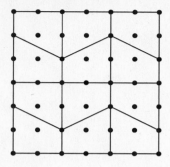

8. *Sample answer:*

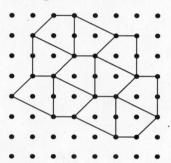

9. Answers vary.

10. Yes; ▭

11. No; all squares are rectangles.

12. No; all rectangles are parallelograms.

13. Yes;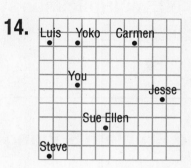

14.

15. Yoko; 3 blocks north

16. Luis and Yoko; 2 blocks

17. 4 blocks west

18. 8 blocks

19. D

20. MATH

21. IS

22. FUN

23. Answers vary.

Answers for Lesson 1.6, pages 29–32

Ongoing Assessment

1. $12 \cdot x = 60$; multiplication symbol does not resemble an x.

2. Answers vary.

Practice and Problem Solving

1. Equation

2. Solution

3. *Sample answer:* Choose n for the *number* of cans.

4. Number of cans; hours per can

5. $t = 336 \times 3\frac{1}{2}$
   $t = 1176$

6. 10

7. 7

8. 6

9. 7

10. 155

11. 23

12. 35

13. 6

14. 4

15. 3

16. 35

17. 32

18. 4

19. $17 - x = 5; x = 12$

20. $5 \cdot x = 40; x = 8$

21. $x \div 2 = 18; x = 36$

22. 8, 6, 4, 2; d decreases by 2.

23. 15, 20, 25, 30; d increases by 5.

24. 5, 6, 7, 8; d increases by 1.

25. 14, 16, 18, 20; d increases by 2.

26. $84 \div n = 7; 12$

27. $s = 350 - 134; 216$

28. $59 + y = 61; 2$ in.

29. $14 + p = 21; 7$ points

30. $m \div 2 = 36; 72$ lengths

(continued)

Answers for Lesson 1.6, pages 29–32(cont.)

31. $180 \div p = 6$; 30 minutes

32. C

33. B

34. **a.** $1 + m = 3.3$; $2.30

    b. $0.1 \times n = 2.3$; 23 people

    c. Answers vary.

35. $p = 800 - 250$;
550 pairs of shoes

Answers for Spiral Review, page 32

1. 53.8

2. 2.21

3. 13.8

4. 13.5

5. 54.73

6. 69.87

7. 16.67

8. 63.15

9. *Sample answer:* 11 in.

10. *Sample answer:* 1 in.

11. *Sample answer:* 7 in.

12. 0.75

13. 0.5

14. 1.0

15. 1.75

16. 3 times

Answers for Lesson 1.7, pages 35–37

Practice and Problem Solving

1. Using inverse operations

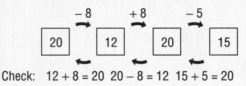

Check: $12 + 8 = 20$ $20 - 8 = 12$ $15 + 5 = 20$

2. What number added to 78 equals 93?
$n = 15; 78 + 15 = 93$

3. What number subtracted from 54 equals 48?
$p = 6; 54 - 6 = 48$

4. What number multiplied by 3 equals 39?
$y = 13; 3 \cdot 13 = 39$

5. 42 divided by what number equals 6?
$b = 7; 42 \div 7 = 6$

6. 9:50 A.M.

7.

```
      ÷8      −4      ×6      +7
  32      4       0       0       7
```
Check: $8 \times 4 = 32$ $0 + 4 = 4$ $0 \div 16 = 0$ $7 - 7 = 0$

8.

```
      ×3      ÷2      −2      +7
  4       12      6       4       11
```
Check: $12 \div 3 = 4$ $6 \times 2 = 12$ $4 + 2 = 6$ $11 - 7 = 4$

9.

```
      +8      ÷5      ×3      −3
  27      35      7       21      18
```
Check: $35 - 8 = 27$ $7 \times 5 = 35$ $21 \div 3 = 7$ $18 + 3 = 21$

10.

```
      +1      ÷6      −9      ×5
  77      78      13      4       20
```
Check: $78 - 1 = 77$ $13 \times 6 = 78$ $4 + 9 = 13$ $20 \div 5 = 4$

11. What number added to 5 equals 24?
$x = 19; 19 + 5 = 24$

(continued)

12. What number subtracted from 18 equals 6?
$y = 12; 18 - 12 = 6$

13. 32 subtracted from what number equals 51?
$a = 83; 83 - 32 = 51$

14. What number added to 6 equals 45?
$n = 39; 6 + 39 = 45$

15. What number added to 55 equals 66?
$t = 11; 11 + 55 = 66$

16. What number subtracted from 68 equals 52?
$d = 16; 68 - 16 = 52$

17. What number multiplied by 8 equals 48?
$b = 6; 8 \cdot 6 = 48$

18. What number divided by 7 equals 10?
$p = 70; 70 \div 7 = 10$

19. What number divided by 8 equals 14?
$c = 112; 112 \div 8 = 14$

20. What number multiplied by 4 equals 112?
$m = 28; 28 \cdot 4 = 112$

21. What number multiplied by 63 equals 189?
$x = 3; 63 \cdot 3 = 189$

22. What number divided into 156 equals 12?
$y = 13; 156 \div 13 = 12$

23. $18 + x = 27; x = 9;$
$18 + 9 = 27$

24. $95 - x = 23; x = 72;$
$95 - 72 = 23$

25. $7 \cdot x = 105; x = 15;$
$15 \cdot 7 = 105$

26. $x \div 4 = 17; x = 68;$
$68 \div 4 = 17$

27. $x \cdot 12 = 60; x = 5$
$5 \cdot 12 = 60$

28. 27

29. 42 m

30. First hole: 2; second hole: 3

31. C

32. D

33. Dolls: 17
Basketball cards: 34
Action figures: 25
Postage stamps: 150
Glass statues: 15

Ongoing Assessment

1. No; the number of pairs is more than double.

2. *Sample answer:* How many different pizzas can be made with a choice of 10 toppings?

Practice and Problem Solving

1. Solve a simpler problem.

2. Draw a diagram.

3. Make a list.

4. Determine how many sit-ups you will do on the second, third, and fourth day to see if any pattern exists.

5. Determine how many rings will be exchanged with 2, 3, and 4 members to see if any pattern exists.

6. 36

7. **a.** 25   **b.** 16   **c.** 3×3: 9   **d.** 55
                                    4×4: 4
                                    5×5: 1

8. The length increases by 4 each time. 60

9.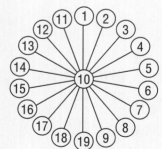

11. A

12.

10. 21

Answers for Spiral Review, page 42

1. 4584

2. 209

3. 1222

4. 8505

5. 13,484

6. 11,752

7. Go on vacation.

8. About 46

9. 14

Answers for Communicating About Mathematics, page 43

1. 85

2. Seagrave Standard

3.

Fire Engine Model	Year	Pumping rate (in gal/min)
Rumsey "Village Fire Engine"	1865	30
Howe/Ford Model T	1918	350
Seagrave Standard	1927	750
Mack Model 1	1951	550

4. About 300; about 50

Answers for Lesson 1.9, pages 45–47

Practice and Problem Solving

1. Draw a Diagram or Using a Graph. Both methods help to visualize the problem.

2. Making a List would help find all the possibilities. Solving a Simpler Problem could also be used.

3. *Sample answer:* Find two consecutive numbers whose sum is 243.

4. Answers vary.

5. **a.** 146, 147   **b.** 26, 27   **c.** 12, 13, 14

6. 13, 37

7. 7 minutes; draw a diagram to find out the number of tape lines needed.

8. 8; Work backward to show the number of cards taken and played.

9. 1990: $4\frac{1}{2}$
   1991: 5
   1992: $4\frac{1}{2}$
   1993: $5\frac{1}{2}$
   1994: $4\frac{1}{2}$

10. 207,000,000; $46,000,000 \times 4.5 = 207,000,000$

(continued)

Answers for Lesson 1.9, pages 45–47 (cont.)

11.

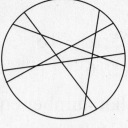

5 cuts, 16 pieces

12. D

13.

	Larry	Myra	Yuki	Manuel
Fancy Spoons	X	O	X	X
Mystery Books	O	X	X	X
Bottle Caps	X	X	X	O
Picture Frames	X	X	O	X

14. Answers vary.

Answers for Chapter Review, pages 49–51

1. Each number increases by
   5, 6, 7, . . .; 61, 70, 80

2. 1993: 629 hours
   1994: 622 hours
   1995: 463 hours

3.

	Broadcast Television	Cable Television
1993	1082	453
1994	1091	469
1995	1019	556
2000	999	651

4. 8

5. 1990

6. About 9 gallons

7. 18

8. 8

9. 54

10. 53

11. $9 + s = 25; s = 16$
    You spent $16.

12. 8 times what number equals
    128? $x = 16$

13. What number divided by 3
    equals 21? $y = 63$

14. What number less 16 equals
    52? $m = 68$

15. First, find the number of
    seconds in a day and then
    multiply this number by 365.

16. 10

17. About 2160 mm

18. 3, 12

Answers for Chapter Assessment, page 52

1. Each number decreases by 1, 3, 5, 7, 9, 11, . . .; 44, 35, 24

2. Each number increases by 1, 2, 3, 4, 5, 6, . . .; 11, 16, 22

3. Each number is multiplied by 2; $\frac{16}{10}, \frac{32}{10}, \frac{64}{10}$

4. List letters in position 1, 4, 7, 10, . . . (an increase of 3 each time); M, P, S

5. 18

6. 49

7. 6

8. 5

9. What number minus 45 equals 110?
155; 155 − 45 = 110

10. What number divided by 3 equals 14?
42; 42 ÷ 3 = 14

11. LT   TK   KM   MP   PY
    LK   TM   KP   MY
    LM   TP   KY
    LP   TY
    LY
There are 15 possible combinations.

12. There are 8 possible triangles.

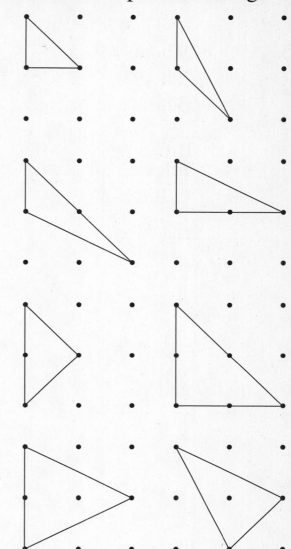

13. Green

14. 7 hours

15. 54 hours

16. 65 hours

17. 1995; people spent 11 more hours watching movies.

Answers for Standardized Test Practice, page 53

1. C
2. B
3. C
4. C

5. D
6. D
7. D
8. B

Answers for Lesson 2.1, pages 61–63

Ongoing Assessment

1. Eight thousand

2. Two hundred ninety-three thousand

3. Ten thousand, nine hundred four

4. One million, two hundred forty thousand, fifty-two

Practice and Problem Solving

1. No; the numbers are grouped by 5's and 10.

2. No; the symbols positions vary. Also, there is no symbol for zero.

3. CCCLXII

4. One hundred two thousand, six hundred eighty-one

5. False; each place gets 10 times larger as you move to the left.

6. True

7. 640

8. 50,307

9. 44,040

10. 2,030,100

11. Five; two

12. One; twenty

13. Three; twenty-five

14. Two; thirty

15. D

16. A

17. C

18. B

19. 865

20. 356

21. 386

22. 536, 538, 563, 568, 583, 586, 635, 638, 653, 658, 683, and 685

(continued)

23. Nova Scotia; ones
New Brunswick; tens
Manitoba; ten thousands
Saskatchewan; ten thousands
British Columbia; tens
Quebec; hundred thousands

24. 30,800

25. 10,759

26. 67,230,000

27. B

28. B

29. ₀· ; fifty

30. ⌈₀⋀ ; three hundred fifty-eight

31. ₀⁹⌈⌈ ; five thousand, nine hundred twenty-two

Answers for Lesson 2.2, pages 67–69

Ongoing Assessment

1. 229   **2.** 501   **3.** 425

Practice and Problem Solving

1. *Sample answer:* Needs regrouping: $273 + 529$
Does not need regrouping: $123 + 456$

2. *Sample answer:* Needs regrouping: $516 - 239$
Does not need regrouping: $456 - 123$

3. 22

4. 32

5. 32

6.
```
  1 3 5
+   6 2
-------
  1 9 7
```

7.
```
  3 8 7
- 1 2 3
-------
  2 6 4
```

8.
```
  1 1
  2 4 3
+   6 8
-------
  3 1 1
```

9.
```
  0 11 15
  1 2 5
-   8 7
-------
    3 8
```

10.
```
  8 17 10
  9 8 0
- 1 9 8
-------
  7 8 2
```

11.
```
  1 1
  7 6 4
+ 3 9 7
-------
1 1 6 1
```

12.
```
  1 1 1
  4 3 2 4
+ 2 9 9 9
---------
  7 3 2 3
```

13.
```
  7 9 9 11
  8 0 0 1
- 5 6 6 7
---------
  2 3 3 4
```

14.
```
  [1] 9 4
+ 3 3 [9]
---------
  5 3 3
```

15.
```
  5 [7] 0
- 2 4 6
---------
 [3] 2 4
```

16.
```
  5 [2] 5 [4]
+ [1] 7 [6] 2
-----------
  7 0 1 6
```

17.
```
  [5] 2 [6] 8
-   [6] 8 [1]
-----------
  4 5 8 7
```

18. $m = 40$

19. $s = 51$

20. $c = 99$

21. $p = 175$

22. $b = 798$

23. $w = 5000$

24. 10 ft

25. 0.4 m

26. 44 cm

27. $35 + 49 = 84$

28. $49 - 16 > 30$

29. $25 - 16 = 9$

30. False

31. False

(continued)

Answers for Lesson 2.2, pages 67–69 (cont.)

32. True

33. B

34. C

35. B

36. Answers vary.

Answers for Spiral Review, page 70

1. 4200

2. 5000

3. 500

4. 25,000

5. 66

6. 72

7. 8

8. 750

9. 4, 8, 12, 16, 20, 24, 28, 32, 36, 40, 44, 48

10. 7, 14, 21, 28, 35, 42, 49

11. 10, 20, 30, 40, 50

12. Ounces

13. Pounds

14. Ounces

15. Tons or pounds

16. Ounces

17. Ounces

18. 7

Answers for Lesson 2.3, pages 73–75

Ongoing Assessment
1. 1332   **2.** 2368

Practice and Problem Solving

1. $7 \times 9 = 63$

2. $4 \times 11 = 44$

3. About 96,250 mi^2

4.

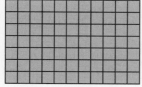

$A = 77$ square units

5. $2 \times 2 = 4$

6. $10 \times 5 = 50$

7. $8 \times 6 = 48$

8. $7 \times 3 = 21$

9.

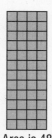

Area is 48
square units.

10.

Area is 121
square units.

11.

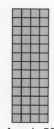

Area is 52
square units.

12.

Area is 45
square units.

13. Bathroom: 27 tiles;
Laundry: 14 tiles;
Hallway: 18 tiles

14. 11

(continued)

Answers for Lesson 2.3, pages 73–75 (cont.)

15. 5

16. 4

17. Even

18. Even

19. Odd

20. 44, 88, 176; pattern: If one of two factors of *n* doubles and the other factor remains constant, then *n* doubles.

21. 2, 4, 8; pattern: If a product doubles and one of its two factors remains constant, then the other factor doubles.

22.

Yes

23. System B

24. C

25. B

26. Total bill is $1870.

Answers for Lesson 2.4, pages 79–82

Ongoing Assessment

1. $4 \text{ R2}; 4\frac{2}{3}$ **2.** $2 \text{ R6}; 2\frac{3}{4}$

3. $16 \text{ R3}; 16\frac{3}{5}$ **4.** $3 \text{ R3}; 3\frac{1}{4}$

Practice and Problem Solving

1. Dividend is 27; divisor is 4.

2.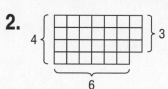

3. $6 \text{ R3}; 6\frac{3}{4}$

4. C; $4 \text{ R1}; 4\frac{1}{3}$

5. A; $2 \text{ R1}; 2\frac{1}{6}$

6. B; $3 \text{ R1}; 3\frac{1}{6}$

7. $52 \div 4; 13$

8. $60 \div 15; 4$

9. $9 \text{ R3}; 9\frac{3}{4}$

10. $8 \text{ R5}; 8\frac{5}{9}$

11. $14 \text{ R1}; 14\frac{1}{3}$

12. $12 \text{ R4}; 12\frac{2}{3}$

13. $23 \text{ R4}; 23\frac{4}{5}$

14. $42 \text{ R2}; 42\frac{2}{3}$

15. $61 \text{ R1}; 61\frac{1}{4}$

16. $27 \text{ R7}; 27\frac{1}{2}$

17. $50 \div 3$

18. $36 \div 5$

19.

$2 \text{ R4}; 2\frac{4}{5}$

20.

$5 \text{ R1}; 5\frac{1}{4}$

21.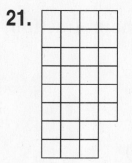

$3 \text{ R6}; 3\frac{3}{4}$

(continued)

22. $5\frac{5}{8}$ cm

23. $7\frac{1}{4}$ ft

24. $140 \div 10 = 14$
$280 \div 10 = 28$
If the divisor is constant, then doubling the dividend doubles the quotient.

25. Your friend probably calculated $45 \div 720$ instead of $720 \div 45$; 16.

26. $9 \div 9 = 1$
$108 \div 9 = 12$
$1107 \div 9 = 123$
$11,106 \div 9 = 1234$
Pattern:
The number of digits in the quotient increases by one.
The new ones' digit of the quotient increases by one.
The number of digits in the dividend increases by one.
The new ones' digit in the dividend decreases by one.
$$111,105 \div 9 = 12,345$$
$$1,111,104 \div 9 = 123,456$$

27. $2\frac{1}{2}$ miles per hour; fraction; refers to fraction of a mile.

28. $2\frac{3}{4}$; dollars per hour; fraction; refers to a fraction of a dollar.

29. C

30. C

31. a. $60 \div 3 = 20$

   b. No, you can ship 20 diskettes in each shipping box. You can ship 7 full boxes. You will have 10 diskettes left over.

Answers for Spiral Review, page 82

1. Perimeter: 34 in.; area: 66 in.^{2}
2. Perimeter: 30 cm; area: 44 cm^2
3. Perimeter: 28 ft; area: 49 ft^2
4. Perimeter: 28 m; area 40 m^2
5. 110
6. 311
7. 70
8. 140
9. 25
10. 2
11. 50
12. 11
13. 70
14. 100
15. 1110
16. 1900
17. 2000
18. 3000

19. Each increases by 8; 27, 35, 43.

20. Each increases by consecutive odd numbers starting with 3; 25, 36, 49

21. $n = 80 \div 15$; $n = 5R5$; remainder; you have 5¢ left over.

Answers for Mid-Chapter Assessment, page 83

1. 41,035

2. 6209

3. 590

4. Four thousand fifty-four

5. Thirty thousand, eight hundred seventy

6. Six hundred fifty-two thousand, one

7. 20

8. 16

9.

10.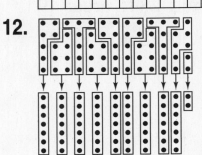

11.

12.

13. 20

14. 36

15. 85

16. 7

17. 4

18. 50

19. About 250 to 300

20. Contemporary; about 500

21. Contemporary; about 800

Answers for Lesson 2.5, pages 85–87

Ongoing Assessment

1. 33; Does not change value: $(32 - 5) + 6 = 33$
   Does change value: $32 - (5 + 6) = 21$

2. 2; Does not change value: $32 - (5 \times 6) = 30$
   Does change value: $(32 - 5) \times 6 = 162$

Practice and Problem Solving

1. B

2. D

3. A

4. C

5. $5 \times (9 - 3) + 12 \div 6 = 32$

6. 21

7. 2

8. 8

9. 56

10. 4

11. 3

12. 18

13. 18

14. 16

15. 50

16. 144

17. 3

18. 100

19. 15

20. 0

21. $(17 - 8) \times 5 = 45$

22. $8 \times 4 + 4 = 36$

23. $25 - 4 \times 5 = 5$

24. *Sample answer:* $4 \times 7 - 2 = 26$

25. *Sample answer:* $7 + 2 \times 9 = 25$

26. *Sample answer:* $4 \times 9 \div 2 = 18$

27. *Sample answer:* $9 + 4 \div 2 = 11$

28. No; $2 + 12 \div 2 \times 3 = 20$

29. $+, \times, -$

30. $+, \times, -$

31. $\times, +, \div$

32. *Sample answer:* $\times, \times, \div$

33. $4 \times 43 + 30 \times 4 \times 2 = \$412$

(continued)

Answers for Lesson 2.5, pages 85–87 (cont.)

34. $700 - (4 \times 43 + 30 \times 4 \times 2) = \$288$

35. $18 \times 20 + 5 = 365$; same

36. B

37. The dirty car drives up.
Water is sprayed on the dirty car.
The car is washed with soapy water.
Soap is rinsed off the car.
The wet car is dried off with towels.
The clean car drives away.

Answers for Lesson 2.6, pages 89–92

Ongoing Assessment
1. 28
2. 30
3. Method 2; Answers vary.

Practice and Problem Solving

1. Without the established order of operations, you will get incorrect answers.

2. $5(6 + 5) = 5 \times 6 + 5 \times 5$
   $$= 30 + 25$$
   $$= 55$$

3. $7(10 + 8) = 7(18)$
   $$= 126$$
   $7(10 + 8) = 7 \times 10 + 7 \times 8$
   $$= 70 + 56$$
   $$= 126$$
   Answers vary.

4. $4 \times 4 = 16; \ 4 \times 2 = 8;$
   $4(4 + 2) = 4 \times 4 + 4 \times 2$
   $$4(6) = 16 + 8$$
   $$24 = 24$$

5. 33
6. 28
7. 54

8. 81
9. 120
10. 147
11. 130
12. 328
13. C; 36; same answer
14. B; 50; same answer
15. D; 56; same answer
16. A; 54; same answer
17. $5(5) = 5(4) + 5(1)$
18. $3(8) = 3(2) + 3(6)$
19. 144
20. 285
21. 371
22. 252
23. $n = 4; \ \ 3 \cdot 10 = 30$
    $$n + 6 = 10$$
    $$n = 4$$

(continued)

24. $x = 4$; $7 \cdot 9 = 63$
$$5 + x = 9$$
$$x = 4$$

25. $y = 4$; $8 \cdot 11 = 88$
$$7 + y = 11$$
$$y = 4$$

26. $a = 3$; $4 \cdot 7 = 28$
$$a + 4 = 7$$
$$a = 3$$

27. $60(70 + 2) = 60(70) + 60(2)$
$$= 4200 + 120$$
$$= 4320 \text{ ft}^2$$

28. $549; no

29. a. $410   **b.** $240

30. D

31. D

32. C

33. C

34. Changing the order does not change the sum.

35. Changing the order does not change the product.

36. Changing the grouping does not change the sum.

37. Changing the grouping does not change the product.

(continued)

38. a. Amount $= 32(22 + 28 + 19)$

$= 32(69)$

$= 2208; \$2208.00$

b.

Meridian Creative Group			
Bill to: Store A			
Game	No.	Price	Cost
Math	22	$32.00	$704.00
Spelling	22	$38.00	$836.00
		Total	**$1540.00**

Meridian Creative Group			
Bill to: Store B			
Game	No.	Price	Cost
Math	28	$32.00	$896.00
Spelling	20	$38.00	$760.00
		Total	**$1656.00**

Meridian Creative Group			
Bill to: Store C			
Game	No.	Price	Cost
Math	19	$32.00	$608.00
Spelling	22	$38.00	$836.00
		Total	**$1444.00**

Answers for Spiral Review, page 92

1. No; *Sample answer:* 5 ft east, 2 ft north, 2 ft west, 7 ft south, 4 ft west, 1 ft south, 8 ft east, 1 ft south

2. 19

3. What number multiplied by 4 equals 60?; $t = 15$

4. What number subtracted from 114 equals 84?; $m = 30$

5. What number minus 32 equals 8?; $g = 40$

6. $14; $7

7. Three hundred twenty-seven

8. Six hundred thousand

9. Fifty-six thousand, four hundred

Answers for Communicating About Mathematics, page 93

1. Numbers 1 and 9 are similar.

2. a. ٤٩

   b. ٢٧٢٢

   c. ٤٤٢٠

3. a. 60

   b. 859

   d. 4201

4. Zero is a placeholder for a place-value system.

5. a. ٩٢

   b. ١٦

   c. ٢٠٧

Answers for Lesson 2.7, pages 97–99

Ongoing Assessment

1. 111_2

2. 11111_2

3. 1100_2

A base-two number is even if the last digit is a 0 and is odd if the last digit is a 1.

Practice and Problem Solving

1. A

2. 302_5

3. 123_5

4. 19

5. 0, 1, 2, 3, 4, and 5

6.

$4^2 = 16$ $4^1 = 4$ $4^0 = 1$

7. Base-five digits are 0, 1, 2, 3, and 4.

8. 37

9. 78

10. 124

11. 232

12. 253

13. 624

14. 102_5

15. 300_5

16. 324_5

17. 1034_5

18. 4100_5

19. 2220_5

20. **a.** 9:41:19 P.M.

   b. *Sample answer:* The concept of time uses base sixty.

21. 9

22. 10

23. 15

24. 26

25. 17

26. 31

27. 1011_2

(continued)

Answers for Lesson 2.7, pages 97–99 (cont.)

28. 10111_2

29. 11111_2

30. 111011_2

31. 27

32. 53

33. 62

34. B

35. C

36. YOU ARE SMART

Answers for Chapter Review, pages 101–103

1. Six hundred eighty thousand, two hundred one

2. $(3 \times 10{,}000) + (5 + 1000) + (7 \times 100) + (9 \times 10)$

3. 5003

4. 672

5. 246

6. 278

7. 21 feet

8. 18 in.

9. $5 \times 2 = 10$

10. 132 ft^2

11. $16 \text{ R}2; 16\frac{1}{3}$

12. $15 \text{ R}1; 15\frac{1}{4}$

13. $9 \text{ R}1; 9\frac{1}{3}$

14. $4 \text{ R}4; 4\frac{1}{3}$

15. 5

16. 23

17. 1

18. 42

19. $5 \times 7 + 4 = \$39$

20. $6(11 + 5) = 6(16)$
$$= 96$$
$6(11 + 5) = 66 + 30$
$$= 96$$

21. 56

22. 96

23. 4

24. 113

25. 30

26. $1111_2; 30_5$

27. $111100_2; 220_5$

28. $100110_2; 123_5$

29. $1011_2; 21_5$

Answers for Chapter Assessment, page 104

1. Five thousand, one hundred ten;
   $(5 \times 1000) + (1 \times 100) + (1 \times 10)$

2. Nineteen thousand, three;
   $(1 \times 10{,}000) + (9 \times 1000) + (3 \times 1)$

3. Three thousand four hundred seventy-two;
   $(3 \times 1000) + (4 \times 100) + (7 \times 10) + (2 \times 1)$

4. Twenty-nine thousand, three hundred eight;
   $(2 \times 10{,}000) + (9 \times 1000) + (3 \times 100) + (8 \times 1)$

5. 835; no

6. 1091; yes

7. 1524; yes

8. 5025; yes

9. $12 \times 5 = 60$

10. $15 \times 4 = 60$

11. 7 R2; $7\frac{2}{5}$

12. 29 R1; $29\frac{1}{3}$

13. 63 R3; $63\frac{3}{4}$

14. 13 R1; $13\frac{1}{2}$

15. 60

16. 42

17. 3

18. 23

19. 616

20. 19

21. 61

22. 15

23. Area: 21 yd^2
    Perimeter: 20 yd

24. 97,000

25. 64,000

Answers for Standardized Test Practice, page 105

1. B

2. B

3. B

4. B

5. D

6. D

7. D

8. C

9. C

10. C

11. B

12. D

Answers for Lesson 3.1, pages 113–115

Ongoing Assessment

1. $(4 \times 1) + (1 \times 0.1)$; 4 large squares and 1 strip

2. $(2 \times 1) + (4 \times 0.1) + (3 \times 0.01)$; 2 large squares, 4 strips, and 3 small squares

3. $(5 \times 1) + (6 \times 0.01)$; 5 large squares and 6 small squares

---

Practice and Problem Solving

1. C

2. B

3. A

4. *Sample answer:* 7000.007

5. 678¢

6. 25¢; $.25

7.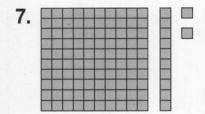

1.12 ones, 11.2 tenths, 112 hundredths

8.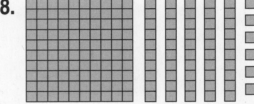

1.56 ones, 15.6 tenths, 156 hundredths

9.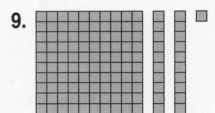

1.21 ones, 12.1 tenths, 121 hundredths

10. *Sample answer:* 1.13 ones, 11.3 tenths

(continued)

Passport to Mathematics Book 1

Answers for Lesson 3.1, pages 113–115 (cont.)

11. *Sample answer:* 5.8 tenths, 58 hundredths
12. *Sample answer:* 2.29 ones, 22.9 tenths
13. Ones
14. Hundredths
15. Tenths
16. 3.4
17. 12.52
18. 0.220
19. 500.03
20. 4.17
21. 0.005
22. $(5 \times 1) + (4 \times 0.1) + (8 \times 0.01)$
23. $(2 \times 10) + (3 \times 1) + (9 \times 0.1) + (3 \times 0.01) + (6 \times 0.001)$
24. $(1 \times 100) + (1 \times 1) + (2 \times 0.01) + (1 \times 0.001)$
25. True
26. False
27. True
28. True
29. $.57, 57¢
30. $11.60, 1160¢
31. $121.00; 12,100¢
32. $1200.00; 120,000¢
33. 5000¢; 5000¢ = $50
34. D
35. A
36. B

Answers for Lesson 3.2, pages 117–119

Ongoing Assessment

1. 2.5 m; *Sample answer:* The width of the bathroom is 2.5 m.

2. 0.25 m; *Sample answer:* Each placemat requires 0.25 m of trim.

3. 4 km; *Sample answer:* Today I jogged 4 km.

4. 20 mm; *Sample answer:* It rained 20 mm in one hour.

Practice and Problem Solving

1. No, the system is based on 12.

2. cm

3. mm

4. cm

5. m

6. Answers vary.

7. 10

8. 10

9. B

10. A

11. D

12. C

13. 1000

14. dm

15. 0.25

16. cm

17. mm

18. 100,000

19. Length: 40mm; width: 20 mm; perimeter: 120 mm

20. Length: 5 cm; width: 2.2 cm; perimeter: 14.4 cm

21. *Sample answer:* 98 cm

22. 0.57 m

23. 6.5 m

24. 280 m

25. 3.6 km

26. 4 mm

27. 10 m

28. <

(continued)

Copyright © McDougal Littell Inc. All rights reserved.

Passport to Mathematics Book 1

Answers for Lesson 3.2, pages 117–119 (cont.)

29. $=$

30. $>$

31. $>$

32. $>$

33. $>$

34. Ornitholestes: 1.8 m
Stegosaurus: 7.6 m
Allosaurus: 9 m
Tyrannosaurus rex: 12 m
Apatosaurus: 21 m

35. The Allosaurus is 5 times as long as the Ornitholestes.

36. D

37. 10,000 km

Answers for Spiral Review, page 120

1. One thousand four hundred thirty-two

2. Eighteen thousand, sixty-seven

3. Nine and fifty-five hundredths

4. Sixteen and forty-three thousandths

5. $(2 \times 1000) + (1 \times 100) + (6 \times 10) + (7 \times 1)$

6. $(8 \times 1000) + (9 \times 10) + (8 \times 1)$

7. $(2 \times 10,000) + (4 \times 100) + (5 \times 10)$

8. $(9 \times 10,000) + (7 \times 1000) + (9 \times 100) + (2 \times 1)$

9. $(3 \times 100,000) + (6 \times 1000) + (5 \times 100) + (2 \times 10)$

10. $(1 \times 1,000,000) + (1 \times 1000) + (1 \times 10)$

11. 14

12. 11

13. 3

14. 120

15. 10

16. 100

17.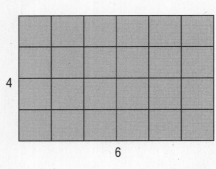

18.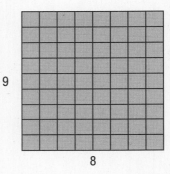

19.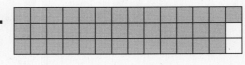

20.

21. $25 + 12(45) = 565$

Answers for Lesson 3.3, pages 125–127

Ongoing Assessment

1. 35 people **2.** 80 people

Practice and Problem Solving

1. 27 hundredths

2. 4 tenths

3. 6 tenths

4. *Sample answer:*

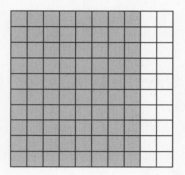

5.

Number-line model

Set model

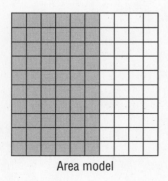

Area model

6.

0   0.2   1.0

7. ▢▢▢▢▢▢▢▢▢□

8.

9. An area model having 100 small squares

10. A set model having 100 circles

11. A number line model from 0 to 1.0

12.

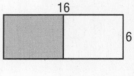

(continued)

Answers for Lesson 3.3, pages 125–127(cont.)

13.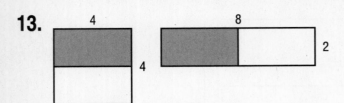

14.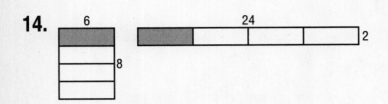

15. $0.3 + 0.5 = 0.8$

16. $0.9 - 0.5 = 0.4$

17. Great Britain: 0.35
Italy: 0.25
Japan: 0.25
Australia: 0.10

18. 25

19. C

20. C

21. $160; travel tips vary.

Answers for Lesson 3.4, pages 129–132

Ongoing Assessment

1. 5%

2. 72%

3. *Sample answer:* What percent are girls who named green?

Practice and Problem Solving

1. 0.56

2. $\frac{56}{100}$

3. 56%

4. Sixty-seven percent

5. Fifteen hundredths

6. Forty-five hundredths

7. 0.5, 50%, $\frac{5}{10}$

8. 0.1, 10%, $\frac{1}{10}$

9. 0.65, $\frac{65}{100}$, 65%

10. 0.50, $\frac{50}{100}$, 50%

11. $\frac{55}{100}$

12. $\frac{18}{100}$

13. $\frac{43}{100}$

14. $\frac{129}{1000}$

15. $\frac{401}{1000}$

16. $\frac{91}{100}$

17. $\frac{49}{10,000}$

18. $\frac{87}{100}$

19. $\frac{39}{100}$

20. 9%

21. True

22. False; $\frac{2}{100} = 2\%, \frac{20}{100} = 20\%$

23. True

24. False; $42\% = \frac{42}{100}, 40.2\% = \frac{402}{1000}$

25. False; $0.01 = 1\%, 0.1 = 10\%$

26. True

27. True

28. False; $99\% = \frac{99}{100}, 99.9\% = \frac{999}{1000}$

(continued)

Answers for Lesson 3.4, pages 129–132 (cont.)

29. 24%

30. 33%

31. 85%

32. 12%

33. 7%

34. 9%

35. 60%

36. 10%

37. $\frac{35}{100}$, 35%

38. $\frac{17}{100}$, 17%

39. $\frac{82}{100}$, 82%

40. $\frac{90}{100}$, 90%

41. 20%

42. 40%

43. 70%

44. 70%

45. D

46. C

47. $9.38

48. **a.** 0.001

    b. $\frac{1}{1000}$

Answers for Spiral Review, page 132

1. 10 sandwiches

2.

3.
$$\begin{array}{r} 2\ \boxed{6}\ 8 \\ -\boxed{1}\ 0\ \boxed{7} \\ \hline 1\ 6\ 1 \end{array}$$

4.
$$\begin{array}{r} 6\ 4\ 7 \\ -4\ \boxed{3}\ \boxed{9} \\ \hline \boxed{2}\ 0\ 8 \end{array}$$

5. $4(5 + 2) = 4(7) = 28$

$4(5 + 2) = 4(5) + 4(2) = 20 + 8 = 28$

6. $3(6 + 7) = 3(13) = 39$

$3(6 + 7) = 3(6) + 3(7) = 18 + 21 = 39$

7. $8(9 + 11) = 8(20) = 160$

$8(9 + 11) = 8(9) + 8(11) = 72 + 88 = 160$

8. $5(4 + 3) = 5(7) = 35$

$5(4 + 3) = 5(4) + 5(3) = 20 + 15 = 35$

9. $7(9 + 2) = 7(11) = 77$

$7(9 + 2) = 7(9) + 7(2) = 63 + 14 = 77$

10. $9(18 + 8) = 9(26) = 234$

$9(18 + 8) = 9(18) + 9(8) = 162 + 72 = 234$

11. cm

12. 30

13. 0.5

14. 2

Answers for Mid-Chapter Assessment, page 133

1.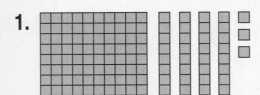

2.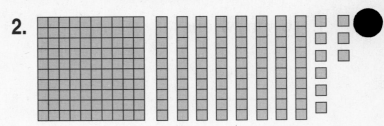

3.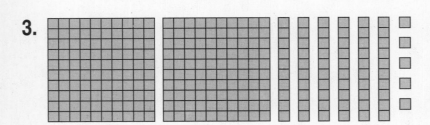

4. 205

5. 0.30

6. 5.15

7. 560

8. m

9. 0.0123

10.
```
|----+----+----+----+----+----+----+----+----+----|
0                        0.7        1.0
```

11.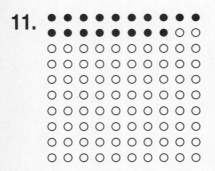

12.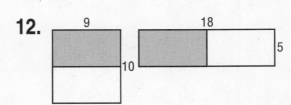

13. 0.6, $\frac{6}{10}$, 60%

14. 0.29, $\frac{29}{100}$, 29%

15. 0.74, $\frac{74}{100}$, 74%

16.

Event	Men's	Women's
High jump	2.45 m	2.09 m
Long jump	8.95 m	7.52 m
Discus	74.1 m	76.8 m

17. Discus

18. VCR: 80%
Cellular phone: 50%
E-mail: 30%

Answers for Lesson 3.5, pages 135–137

Ongoing Assessment

1. >   2. <   3. >   4. >

Practice and Problem Solving

1. A: 1.6, B: 2.1, C: 1.1,
   D: 0.2, E: 0.8

2.
```
0.6 0.61 0.62 0.63 0.64 0.65 0.66 0.67 0.68 0.69 0.7
```
   0.68, 0.69, 0.7

3. *Sample answer:*
   6.51, 6.56, 6.59

4. 0.04, 0.4, 0.45, 0.5, 0.54

5. 0.02, 0.2, 0.25, 0.5, 2.5

6. 0.07, 0.10, 0.17, 0.7, 1.7

7. 6.08, 6.12, 6.18, 6.8, 6.82

8. 4.03, 4.1, 4.13, 4.39, 4.4

9. 0.026, 0.06, 0.126, 0.2, 0.26

10. 5.1, 5.104, 5.13, 5.14, 5.143

11. 1.107, 1.69, 1.709, 1.76, 1.9

12. 4.081, 4.118, 4.18, 4.218, 4.281

13. >   17. =
14. <   18. <
15. <   19. =
16. >   20. >

21. C, A, B, E, D

22. E

23. C

24. D is twice as long as A.

25. B is four times as long as C.

26. 0.23

27. 0.2

28. 0.3

29. 0.2, 0.23, 0.3

30.
```
3.2 3.21 3.22 3.23 3.24 3.25 3.26 3.27 3.28 3.29 3.3
```
   Hundredths

31. 917.2, 917.203, 917.22,
    917.26, 917.267

32. A

33.
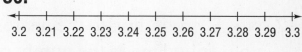

Answers for Lesson 3.6, pages 139–142

Practice and Problem Solving

1. *Sample answer:* When determining interest earned in a bank account; when deciding how to divide a lunch bill among friends

2. *Sample answer:*

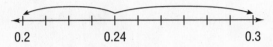

   0.24 is closer to 0.2 than it is to 0.3.

3. 4.524

4. 4.52

5. 4.5

6. 5

7. No. By rounding to the nearest hundredth first, your friend made the number seem larger than it is.

8.

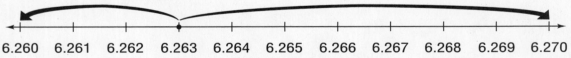

   6.263 is closer to 6.26.

9.

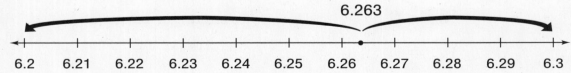

   6.263 is closer to 6.3.

(continued)

10.

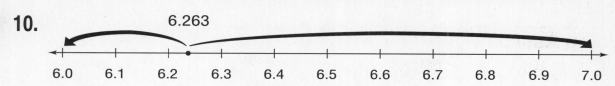

6.263

6.0 6.1 6.2 6.3 6.4 6.5 6.6 6.7 6.8 6.9 7.0

6.263 is closer to 6.0.

11. 270

12. 35,000

13. 412,000

14. 5.4

15. 21

16. 8.517

17. True

18. True

19. False; 5.4

20. True

21. 22,000

22. 99

23. 80

24. $32.00

25. $25.00

26. $612.00

27. $2.00

28. $89.00

29. $95.00

30. $9.00

31. $67.00

32. $21.00

33. Penny: 0.7
Nickel: 2.7
Dime: 1.6

34. 3, acid

35. 9, base

36. 8, base

37. 2, acid

38. 4, acid

39. 7, acid

40. 16

41. 14

42. 88

43. 41

44. 41

45. 7

46. 22

47. 7

48. 3

(continued)

Answers for Lesson 3.6, pages 139–142 (cont.)

49. 6.4

50. 8.6

51. 53.1°

52. 36.9°

53. B

54. C

55. 1996 and 1997; yes, the number of rupees per dollar has been increasing.

Answers for Spiral Review, page 142

1. Lee, Chris, Pat;
Lee, Pat, Chris;
Chris, Pat, Lee;
Chris, Lee, Pat;
Pat, Lee, Chris;
Pat, Chris, Lee

2. 7 R1 or $7\frac{1}{2}$

3. 8 R1 or $8\frac{1}{4}$

4. 24 R1 or $24\frac{1}{5}$

5. 24 R4 or $24\frac{4}{9}$

6. 12

7. 8

8. 3

9. 12

10. 8

11. 109

12. 13

13. 27

14. 1.5

15. 4.57

16. 100.01

17. 10.050

18. 12

Answers for Communicating About Mathematics, page 143

1. 40%; $\frac{2}{5} = \frac{4}{10} = \frac{40}{100}$, or 40%

2. 400 pictures; $\frac{2}{5}(1000) = 400$

3. *Sample answer:* The technology and its upkeep are costly; data might be about car speed, force of impact, or position of dummy.

4.
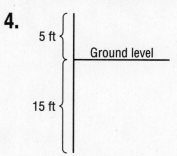

The entire wall is 20 ft; $\frac{15}{20} = \frac{75}{100}$, or 75%.

5. a. $520 \text{ ft} \times \frac{1 \text{ mile}}{5280 \text{ ft}} \approx 0.1 \text{ mile}$

   b. $520 \text{ ft} \times \frac{1 \text{ mile}}{5280 \text{ ft}} \approx \frac{1}{10} \text{ mile}$

Answers for Lesson 3.7, pages 145–147

Ongoing Assessment

1. 8   **2.** 8   **2.** 5

Practice and Problem Solving

1. 22

2. 6

3. 22^6

4. 100; 1000; 10,000; 100,000; 1,000,000

5. $(2 \times 10^3) + (9 \times 10^2) + (9 \times 10) + (3 \times 1)$

6. False; 9

7. 2

8. 4

9. 3

10. 3

11. 9

12. 4

13. 2

14. 10

15. 625

16. 729

17. 729

18. $\frac{1}{10,000}$

19. $\frac{1}{1,000,000}$

20. 343

21. 12,167

22. 15,625

23. 14,641

24. 125,000

25. 43,046,721

26. 1,048,576

27. 3,748,096

28. 1,679,616

29. $(7 \times 10) + (5 \times 1)$

30. $(3 \times 10^2) + (8 \times 10)$

31. $(1 \times 10^3) + (3 \times 10)$

32. $(2 \times 10^3) + (8 \times 10)$

33. 49; 50

34. 125; 130

35. 2197; 2200

(continued)

Answers for Lesson 3.7, pages 145–147 (cont.)

36. 576; 580

37. 8 cm

38. 7 in.

39. 10 mm

40. 11 ft

41. 10^2

42. 10^3

43. 27

44. 170

45. 7

46. 130

47. 84

48. 1728; 12^3

49. C

50. C

51. Your friend

Answers for Lesson 3.8, pages 149–151

Ongoing Assessment

1. 0.3, $\frac{3}{10}$, 30%

2. 0.2, $\frac{1}{5}$, 20%

Practice and Problem Solving

1. 390

2.

3. 0.4, $\frac{4}{10}$, 40%

4. 0.25, $\frac{25}{100}$, 25%

5. 0.35, $\frac{35}{100}$, 35%

6. 0.4, $\frac{4}{10}$, 40%

7. 0.6, $\frac{6}{10}$, 60%

8.

14

9.

$9.00

10. 45

11. 200

12. 48

13. A: 20; B: 15, C: 10, D: 5

14. 0.75, $\frac{75}{100}$, 75% - pennies

0.05, $\frac{5}{100}$, 5% - nickels

0.1, $\frac{1}{10}$, 10% - dimes

0.1 $\frac{1}{10}$, 10% - quarters

15. Yes, 55% of 200 is 110.

16. C

17. A

18. 1330 drachmas or $5 per souvenir

Answers for Chapter Review, pages 153–155

1. Fifteen and ninety-two hundredths

2. Four and sixty-seven thousandths

3. $(5 \times 100) + (4 \times 10) + (1 \times 1) + (9 \times 0.1) + (9 \times 0.01)$

4. $(3 \times 10) + (1 \times 0.1) + (8 \times 0.001)$

5. Kilometers

6. 50

7. 5.2

8. 0.017

9. 20m; 2000 cm; 20,000 mm

10.

11. 0.8

12. $\frac{897}{1000}$

13. $\frac{81}{100}$

14. 47%

15. 0.227

16. 10.97 > 10.94 so 1996's time is faster.

17. 10.54, 10.82, 10.94, 10.97, 11.06

18. $4.00, $4.00, $4.00, $2.00, $1.00

19. 216

20. 729

21. 79

22. 39 people

23. 18 books

24. 50 pages

Answers for Chapter Assessment, page 156

1. 6.9

2. 14.05

3. 0.612

4. 300.03

5. 14.5

6. 3

7. 0.205

8. 71

9. 6

10.

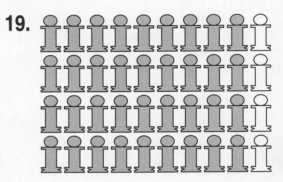

0   0.7   1.0

11.

12. 6.019, 6.109, 6.129, 6.19, 6.2

13. 32.08, 32.89, 32.94, 33.09, 33.90

14. 0.04, 0.08, 0.08, 0.12, 0.14, 0.15

15. 4%, 8%, 8%, 12%, 14%, 15%

16. 26

17. 9

18. 36

19.

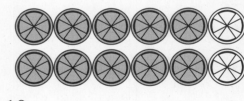

36

20.

10

Answers for Standardized Test Practice, page 157

1. C

2. B

3. B

4. A

5. B

6. C

7. C

8. D

9. C

10. A

11. C

12. A

13. C

14. C

Answers for Cumulative Review, pages 158 and 159

1. Perimeter: 4, 6, 8, 10, 12, 14
Area: 1, 2, 3, 4, 5, 6
Perimeters increase by 2.
Areas increase by 1.

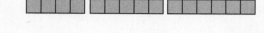

2. Perimeter: 4, 12, 20, 28, 36, 44
Area: 1, 5, 9, 13, 17, 21
Perimeters increase by 8.
Areas increase by 4.

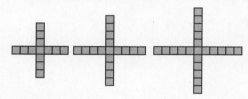

3. Not possible because all parallelograms are quadrilaterals.

4. *Sample answer:*

5. 26

6. 4

7. 27

8. 240

9. 6

10. 3

11. | 10 | 70 | 14 | 8 | 16 |

12. | 52 | 45 | 15 | 19 | 38 |

13. 815

14. 392

15. 57.5

16. Strips

17. Small squares

18. 20

19. 25

20. 28

21. 60; $(4 \times 9) + (4 \times 6)$ or 4×15

22. 66; $(3 \times 12) + (3 \times 10)$ or 3×22

23. 140; $(7 \times 8) + (7 \times 12)$ or 7×20

24. 45; $(3 \times 13) + (3 \times 2)$ or 3×15

25.

(continued)

Answers for Cumulative Review, pages 158 and 159 (cont.)

26.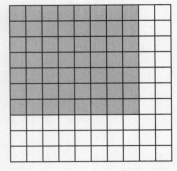

27. True, $\frac{9}{10} = \frac{90}{100} = 90\%$

28. False, $30\% = \frac{30}{100}$

29. False, $\frac{8}{10} = 0.8$

30. True, $\frac{70}{100} = \frac{7}{10} = 0.7$

31. 6.9

32. 25

33. 8000

34. ttt, tth, tht, htt, thh, hth, hht, hhh

35. Magic: 73%; Knicks: 57%; Heat: 51%; Bullets: 48%; Celtics: 10%

36. 0.10, 0.73, 0.57, 0.48, 0.51

37. 0.10, 0.48, 0.51, 0.57, 0.73

38. 0.1, 0.7, 0.6, 0.5, 0.5

39. 5 weeks

Answers for Lesson 4.1, pages 167–169

<table>
<tr><td colspan="2">Ongoing Assessment</td></tr>
</table>

Ongoing Assessment

1.
$$\begin{array}{r} 0.360 \\ + 1.082 \\ \hline 1.442 \end{array}$$

2.
$$\begin{array}{r} 2.508 \\ + 31.110 \\ \hline 33.618 \end{array}$$

3.
$$\begin{array}{r} 9.005 \\ + 0.046 \\ \hline 9.051 \end{array}$$

Practice and Problem Solving

1.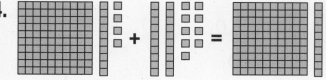

$$\begin{array}{r} 2.45 \\ + 2.38 \\ \hline 4.83 \end{array}$$

2. Decimal points are not aligned.

$$\begin{array}{r} 16.0 \\ + 0.4 \\ \hline 16.4 \end{array} \qquad \begin{array}{r} 1.6 \\ + 0.4 \\ \hline 2.0 \end{array}$$

3. *Sample answer:* $4.22 + 6.23 = 10.45$

4.

$$\begin{array}{r} 1.14 \\ + 0.29 \\ \hline 1.43 \end{array}$$

5.

$$\begin{array}{r} 1.23 \\ + 0.36 \\ \hline 1.59 \end{array}$$

6.
$$\begin{array}{r} 6.87 \\ + 7.24 \\ \hline 14.11 \end{array}$$

7.
$$\begin{array}{r} 0.30 \\ + 9.06 \\ \hline 9.36 \end{array}$$

(continued)

8.
$$
\begin{array}{r}
0.08 \\
+8.00 \\
\hline
8.08
\end{array}
$$

9.
$$
\begin{array}{r}
13.60 \\
0.95 \\
+ 2.2 \\
\hline
16.75
\end{array}
$$

10.
$$
\begin{array}{r}
3.8\boxed{0} \\
+ 0.\boxed{1}5 \\
\hline
\boxed{3}.9\,5
\end{array}
$$

11.
$$
\begin{array}{r}
\boxed{6}.0\,7 \\
+ 3.\boxed{8}\boxed{4} \\
\hline
9.9\,1
\end{array}
$$

12.
$$
\begin{array}{r}
4.\boxed{8}\boxed{7} \\
+ 0.5\,0 \\
\hline
\boxed{5}.3\,7
\end{array}
$$

13.
$$
\begin{array}{r}
\boxed{4}.2\,0 \\
+ 2.\boxed{1} \\
\hline
6.3\,0
\end{array}
$$

14. $x = 48$

15. $y = 31$

16. $z = 9$

17. 18.94 m

18. 5.82 cm

19. 122.312, 123.423, 124.534
Sums increase by 1.111.
$31.345 + 94.3 = 125.645$
$32.456 + 94.3 = 126.756$

20. 1111, 2222, 3333
Sums increase by 1111.
$878.78 + 3565.22 = 4444$
$989.89 + 4565.11 = 5555$

21.

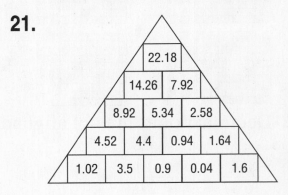

22. 267.06; you won the silver medal.

23. 3.02

24. D

25. Answers vary.

Answers for Lesson 4.2, pages 171–173

Ongoing Assessment

1. Decimals not lined up.

$$\begin{array}{r} 3.20 \\ - \ 1.78 \\ \hline 1.42 \end{array}$$

Align the decimals.

2. Decimals not lined up.

$$\begin{array}{r} 4.73 \\ - \ 2.10 \\ \hline 2.63 \end{array}$$

Align the decimals.

Practice and Problem Solving

1. $2.45 - 2.38 = 0.07$

2. Incorrect

$$\begin{array}{r} 0.86 \\ - \ 0.20 \\ \hline 0.66 \end{array}$$

3. Correct

$$\begin{array}{r} 3.00 \\ - \ 2.85 \\ \hline 0.15 \end{array}$$

4. Incorrect

$$\begin{array}{r} 10.50 \\ - \ \ \ .82 \\ \hline 9.68 \end{array}$$

5.
$$\begin{array}{r} 1.01 \\ - \ 0.34 \\ \hline 0.67 \end{array}$$

6.
$$\begin{array}{r} 0.46 \\ - \ 0.28 \\ \hline 0.18 \end{array}$$

7. B;
$$\begin{array}{r} 2.00 \\ - \ 0.81 \\ \hline 1.19 \end{array}$$

8.
$$\begin{array}{r} 12.21 \\ - 10.50 \\ \hline 1.71\% \end{array}$$

9.
$$\begin{array}{r} 11.31 \\ - \ \ 8.62 \\ \hline 2.69\% \end{array}$$

10. Men: 68.07%; women: 90.25%; some people who are 18–24 years old are shorter than 5′2″ and some are taller than 5′11″.

11.
$$\begin{array}{r} 6.75 \\ - \ 2.30 \\ \hline 4.45 \end{array}$$

12.
$$\begin{array}{r} 4.33 \\ - \ 3.90 \\ \hline 0.43 \end{array}$$

(continued)

Answers for Lesson 4.2, pages 171–173 (cont.)

13.
$$\begin{array}{r} 7.619 \\ -\,3.800 \\ \hline 3.819 \end{array}$$

14.
$$\begin{array}{r} 5.452 \\ -\,2.910 \\ \hline 2.542 \end{array}$$

15.
$$\begin{array}{r} 5.00 \\ -\,2.89 \\ \hline 2.11 \end{array}$$

16.
$$\begin{array}{r} 12.000 \\ -\,7.652 \\ \hline 4.348 \end{array}$$

17.
$$\begin{array}{r} 0.88 \\ -\,0.39 \\ \hline 0.49 \end{array}$$

18.
$$\begin{array}{r} 1.250 \\ -\,0.056 \\ \hline 1.194 \end{array}$$

19. 3.302

20. 10.992

21. 5.697

22. 7.683

23. Pacific; East Central; $20.1 - 4.4 = 15.7$ gallons per person

24. $16.4 - 11.3 = 5.1$ gallons per person

25. Answers vary.

26. No; $20.00 - $10.80 = $9.20

27. Yes

28. B

29. Answers vary.

Answers for Spiral Review, page 174

1. Denominator increases by 3; $\frac{1}{12}$, $\frac{1}{15}$, $\frac{1}{18}$

2. Each number increases by 0.25; 10.00, 10.25, 10.50

3.
```
  4̲6̲9̲
+ 1 3̲ 5
─────
  6 0 4
```

4.
```
  6 5 5̲
− 3 7̲ 7
─────
  2̲ 7 8
```

5.
```
      8̲ 9
×     2̲
─────
  1̲ 7 8
```

6.
```
       3 8̲
1̲2̲)̄4̄5̄6̄
```

7. Three thousand two hundred twelve

8. 7.1

9. 170

10. 23.18

11. 125 blocks, 5^3

Answers for Lesson 4.3, pages 177–179

Ongoing Assessment

1. *Sample answer:* Estimate the amount of time needed to cut several lawns.

2. *Sample answer:* Estimate the cost of lunch at a fast food restaurant.

Practice and Problem Solving

1. Rounding and front-end estimation; answers vary.
2. 9
3. 13.02
4. 20,000
5. 60
6. 2.6
7. 700
8. 4 games
9. 100
10. 900
11. 9300
12. 900
13. 2900
14. 100
15. $25.00; $25.50
16. $12.00; $12.50
17. $12.00; $12.50
18. $23.00; $23.50
19. $9.00; $8.00
20. $196.00; $195.00
21. 300; 440
22. 2.0; 2.2
23. 0; 60
24. 70; 80
25. 1000; 1700
26. 5000; 6400
27. 9 units
28. 16 units
29. 5 units
30. Buy the rounded tank; about $2.00
31. 3 sets

(continued)

Answers for Lesson 4.3, pages 177–179 (cont.)

32. Week 1: about $12.00
Week 2: about $12.00
Week 3: about $2.00
Total savings: about $26.00

33. D

34. a.–c. Answers vary.

Answers for Lesson 4.4, pages 183–186

Ongoing Assessment	
1. $827.00	**2.** $3.98

Practice and Problem Solving

1. 3

2. 5

3. 6

4. 22

5. 176

6. 176

7. C; it's a little more than 50×2.

8. D; it's about half of 0.235.

9. B; because $5 \times 0.2 = 1$.

10. A; it's close to 5×2.

11. 10.25

12. 189.503

13. 16.1001

14. 11.8440

15. 400, 1000, 1600, 1800, 1900, 1980; the product gets closer to 2000.

16. 3

17. 3

18. 4.4

19. 3.77 mm^2

20. 0.7225 km^2

21. 0.80064 cm^2

22. 12.6225

23. 1.43787

24. 6.62625

25. 0.6176

26. 9.931285

27. 0.299268

28. 2.4625

29. 72.7824

30. 0.102

31. 10.16 cm

32. 17.526 cm

33. 1.016 cm

34. 1.42494 cm

35. 50.8 cm

36. 0.254 cm

(continued)

Answers for Lesson 4.4, pages 183–186 (cont.)

37. 30.48 cm

38. 76.2 cm

39. $0.3 \times 6 = 1.8$

40. $0.12 \times 80 = 9.6$

41. $0.48 \times 6.75 = 3.24$

42. $0.74 \times 74 = 54.76$

43. $0.43 \times 9.5 = 4.085$

44. $0.9 \times 8.1 = 7.29$

45. $683.60

46. $2.74

47. C

48. D

49. B

50. Multiply the amount of the bill by 0.15 to get the amount of tip; tip for this check is $(3.00 + 1.25 + 2.60 + 1.50) \times 0.15 \approx \$1.25$; bill for $2.00 tip will be about $13.35; bill for $5.00 tip will be about $33.35.

51. $12.50

Answers for Spiral Review, page 186

1. 18

2. 9

3. 10

4. 64

5. $27 - (9 - 4) + 2 = 24$

6. $(8 + 2) \times 6 \div 4 = 15$

7. $12 \div (6 + 6) \times 7 = 7$

8. 1.02, 1.03, 1.13, 1.30

9. 9.4, 9.45, 9.5, 9.54

10. 81

11. 3

12. 2

13. 5

14.–16. Answers vary.

17. 57 students; 93 students

Answers for Mid-Chapter Assessment, page 187

1. 9.23

2. $4.43

3. 3.95

4. 9.18

5. 11.62

6. $24.27

7.–9. Answers vary.

7. About $11.00; front-end or rounding

8. About 26,000; front-end or rounding

9. About $29.00; front-end or rounding

10. 3.5

11. 4.56

12. 35.90

13. 3.06

14. 0.54

15. 0.05

16. 12.57 units

17. 33.6 units

18. 36.48 square units

19. $0.8 \times 75 = 60$

20. $0.5 \times 37 = 18.5$

21. $0.35 \times 46 = 16.1$

22. about $7; ice cream

23. spaghetti, Caesar salad, iced tea, and pie, *or* lasagna, garden salad, soda, and pie; Guess, check, and revise

24. $11.67

Answers for Lesson 4.5, pages 189–191

Ongoing Assessment

1. Answers vary.

2. Answers vary.

Practice and Problem Solving

1. $3.42 \div 3 = 1.14$

2.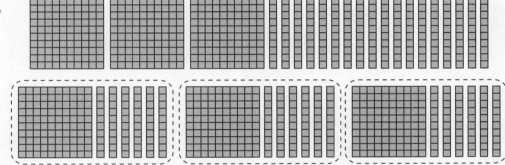

1.6

3. *Sample answer:* Place the decimal number in the division box and the whole number to the left of the curved line. Divide as though you were dividing one whole number by another. After you find a quotient, locate the decimal point in your answer by inserting it directly above the decimal point in the division box.

(continued)

4. About 3;

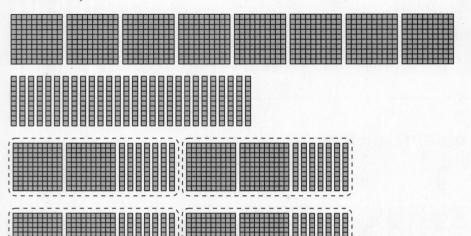

$$\begin{array}{r} 2.7 \\ 4\overline{)10.8} \\ \underline{8} \\ 28 \\ \underline{28} \\ 0 \end{array}$$

5. About 3;

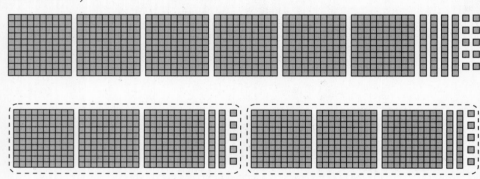

$$\begin{array}{r} 3.25 \\ 2\overline{)6.50} \\ \underline{6} \\ 5 \\ \underline{4} \\ 10 \\ \underline{10} \\ 0 \end{array}$$

6. About 3;

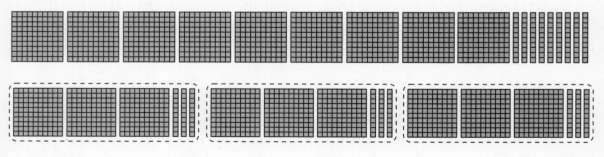

$$\begin{array}{r} 3.3 \\ 3\overline{)9.9} \\ \underline{9} \\ 9 \\ \underline{9} \\ 0 \end{array}$$

(continued)

Answers for Lesson 4.5, pages 189–191 (cont.)

7. About 1;

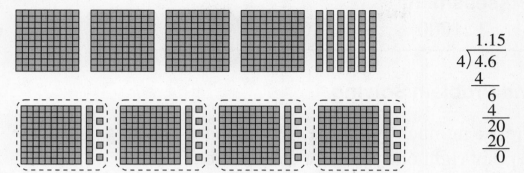

$$\begin{array}{r} 1.15 \\ 4\overline{)4.6} \\ \underline{4} \\ 6 \\ \underline{4} \\ 20 \\ \underline{20} \\ 0 \end{array}$$

8. $1.36 \div 4 = 0.34$

9. $3.9 \div 3 = 1.3$

10. 1.65

11. 5.8

12. 16.7

13. 4.78

14. 9

15. 3

16. 10

17. The quotient is halved.

18. The 8 should be placed above the 6. Correct answer is 8.03.

19. Never; $0.9 \div 2 = 0.45$

20. Always; $5.1 \div 3 = 1.7$

21. $1.45 per week

22. Newspapers: $4.07
Magazines: $3.01
Books: $6.72

23. Books

24. 9.48 in. by 9.48 in.

25. D

26. Answers vary.

Answers for Lesson 4.6, pages 193–196

Ongoing Assessment

1. 100   **2.** 1000   **3.** 10   **4.** 100

Practice and Problem Solving

1. To multiply a number by a power of ten, move the decimal point right one place for each power. To divide, move the decimal left one place for each power. Answers vary.

2. Answers vary. Multiplying makes a number bigger so the decimal point moves right.

3. 4.2	**16.** 32	**29.** 40
4. 0.056	**17.** 0.004	**30.** 3,750,000,000
5. 1.7	**18.** 0.004	**31.** 10
6. 8300	**19.** 79.9	**32.** 0.039
7. 9000	**20.** 0.0046	**33.** 518
8. 85,000	**21.** 0.462	**34.** 1000
9. 230	**22.** 0.8	**35.** 1000
10. 6300	**23.** 0.52	**36.** 987.6
11. 23.7	**24.** 548	**37.** >
12. 1.9	**25.** 18,000	**38.** >
13. 1200	**26.** 2000	**39.** <
14. 145,000	**27.** 250	**40.** =
15. 110,000	**28.** 220,000	**41.** <

(continued)

42. >

43. 6.4 acres

44. 25,000,000,000,000; 12

45. a. 50,000,000,000,000
   b. 100,000,000,000; 0.2%

46. A

47. C

48. B

49. Monaco: 32,000; Figi: 780,000; Zambia: 9,200,000;
   Mexico: 96,000,000; U.S.: 270,000,000;
   China: 1,200,000,000

Answers for Spiral Review, page 196

1. 52

2. $\frac{9}{100}$

3. 6%

4. ÷

5. −

6. =

7. <

8. >

9. 64

10. 243

11. 216

12. 256

Answers for Communicating About Mathematics, page 197

1. 42,500,000 bales

2. $\frac{7}{21,257}$

3. 0.5 bales;

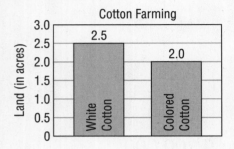

Cotton Farming

4. $1875

5. 10.7% of the colored cotton grown in the United States is grown on Sally Fox's fields.

Answers for Lesson 4.7, pages 201–203

Ongoing Assessment

1.–2. Answers vary.

Practice and Problem Solving

1. You don't know the quotient before dividing. Change "quotient" to "divisor".

2. Moving a decimal point two places to the right is the same as multiplying by 100. Change "1000" to "100" or change "two" to "three".

3. 22

4. 2.2

5. 220

6. 0.22

7. 10

8. 10^2 or 100

9. 10^2 or 100

10. 10^3 or 1000

11. 13

12. 0.4

13. 15.7

14. 300

15. 11.25

16. 1.2

17. 1570

18. 40.4

19. 2000

20. 203.34

21. 219

22. 1375

23. 4.5 m

24. 2.5 km

25. Carrot: 15.6 lb
Onion: 12.4 lb
Pumpkin: 997.8 lb
Cucumber: 20.2 lb
Radish: 38.2 lb
Zucchini: 65.1 lb

26. 0.65; 0.065

27. 20; 200

28. 100; 1000

29. $5.38 per meter

30. $1.34 per meter

(continued)

Answers for Lesson 4.7, pages 201–203 (cont.)

31. $8.07 per meter

32. A

33. C

34. The item with the lowest price per ounce is the better buy; the 16 oz soup and the 48 oz spaghetti are the best buys.

Answers for Lesson 4.8, pages 205–207

Ongoing Assessment

1. 15   **2.** 30   **3.** 18

Practice and Problem Solving

1. B

2. C

3. A

4. 84

5. 30

6. Answers vary.

7. 24

8. 68.75

9. 36

10. 255

11. $15.00; $22.50

12. $1.60; $6.40

13. $1.00; $5.00

14. $5.40 per hour

15. 5,000,000

16. 2,500,000

17. 500,000

18. 84

19. 54

20. 45

21. 33

22. 1,909,830

23. 852,390

24. 1,173,120

25. 768,180

26. C

27. A

28.

Employee	Total Pay	Estimated Take-home Pay
Sonya	$339.20	$271.36
Tom	$317.63	$254.10
Alicia	$140.88	$112.70
Luis	$106.38	$85.10

Answers for Chapter Review, pages 209–211

1. $1.80
2. Notebook and pen
3. $.96
4. 0.38 oz
5. $38.50; $30
6. $7.00; $10
7. $12.00; $11.00
8. $7.50; $7.00
9. $360.50; $300
10. $161.50; $200
11. No
12. No
13. 55.822
14. 3.6
15. 78
16. 32
17. Pigeon: 1.609 km/min
    Monarch Butterfly: 0.536 km/min
    Honeybee: 0.268 km/min

18. 0.23 pound/month
19. 27,500
20. 0.01455
21. $3.17
22. 5 m
23. 36.125
24. 31
25. 42.6
26. 19,100
27. 18.4
28. 22.3
29. $6.60
30. $40.50
31. 100 units: $11.50
    500 units: $50.43
    1000 units: $91.25

Answers for Chapter Assessment, page 212

1. 10.47
2. 10.23
3. 9.951
4. 11.021
5. 21.525
6. 5.85
7. 10.0125
8. 7.2
9. 13.1 mi
10. 10.53 sq ft
11. 4.63 in.
12. >
13. =
14. >
15. <
16. 48
17. 42
18. 52
19. 50.44 lb
20. 64.02 lb
21. 1.29 lb per month
22. Chicken and pork
23. Local sercice: $19.22
    Long distance service: $42.78
24. The science fiction book; the sale prices for the science fiction book and the mystery book are $5.00 and $5.25, respectively.

Answers for Standardized Test Practice, page 213

1. A
2. C
3. C
4. A
5. B
6. C
7. B
8. C
9. D

Answers for Lesson 5.1, pages 221–223

Ongoing Assessment

1. 54 salmon

2. 7 pounds

3. *Sample answer:* Most sockeyes weigh 5 to 7 pounds, while most cohos weigh 8 to 10 pounds. Few sockeyes weigh more than 8 pounds. Few cohos weigh less than 8 pounds.

Practice and Problem Solving

1. A

2. C

3. B

4. Answers vary.

5.

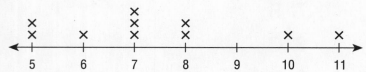

6. Range: $19 - 6 = 13; 8$

7.

Most common number: 7
Smallest number: 5
Largest number: 11
Range: $11 - 5 = 6$

(continued)

8.

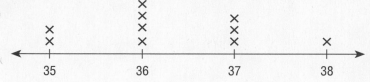

Most common number: 36
Smallest number: 35
Largest number: 38
Range: $38 - 35 = 3$

9.

Most common number: 1.6
Smallest number: 1.1
Largest number: 1.7
Range: $1.7 - 1.1 = 0.6$

10. 34 and 42

11. *Sample answer:* Meat-eating mammals have a tooth on the left side for each tooth on the right side of the mouth.

12.

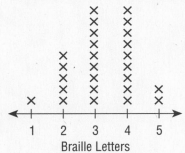

Braille Letters

13. 3 and 4

14. *Sample answer:* (1) Range is 4.
(2) Largest number is 5, smallest is 1.

(continued)

15.

Number of Colors in Flags

Range: 3

16. Line plots vary.

17. D

18. Answers vary.

Answers for Lesson 5.2, pages 225–227

Ongoing Assessment

1. 21, 31, 39, 44, 45, 47, 48, 49, 49, 50, 52, 54, 56, 56, 56, 56, 59, 60, 60, 63

2. *Sample answers:* What is the most common age? Who was the oldest First Lady? Have there been more First Ladies in their forties or in their fifties?

3. Answers vary.

Practice and Problem Solving

1. The stem should represent the higher place values in the numbers of the data. Write these values in ascending order to the left of the stem with their corresponding lower values in a row across from them on the right. Each value on the left should be listed only once, but the values on the right should be repeated each time they occur. Arrange each row of numbers on the right in ascending order. The column on the left forms the stem and the rows on the right are the leaves.

2.

0	1 2 5
1	0 1 4 6 8
2	1 2 6 7 9
3	3 3 5 9

Key: 1 | 6 = 16

Order: 1, 2, 5, 10, 11, 14, 16, 18, 21, 22, 26, 27, 29, 33, 33, 35, 39

3. 7.1, 7.2, 7.7, 8.2, 8.5, 8.6, 8.8, 8.9, 9.0, 9.3, 9.4, 9.4, 9.8

4. C

5. B

6. A

7. 3, 4, 5

8. *Sample answer:*
Key: 1 | 7 = 17; no, many other keys would be equally appropriate.

(continued)

Answers for Lesson 5.2, pages 225–227 (cont.)

9.

0	2 3 5 9
1	0 5 6 7
2	3 4
3	0 1 1 4 8 9
4	2
5	6 9 9

Key: 1 | 7 = 17

10.

5	8 9
6	2 2 3 4 4 4 4 5 5 6 6 8 9
7	0 0 0 0 1 1 1 2

Key: 7 | 0 = 70

11. Record Highs in December

6	8 9
7	0 3 4 4 4 5 7 7
8	0 1 3 4 4 5 5
9	0 4

Key: 7 | 3 = 73

12. Texas

13. 74°F

14.

0	4 6 8 8
1	0 0 2 2 4 6

Key: 1 | 2 = 12

15. C

16. C

17. Answers vary.

Answers for Spiral Review, page 228

1. $5 + x = 27$
   $x = 22$

2. $4 \cdot x = 48$
   $x = 12$

3. $3205 = 3(1000) + 2(100) + 5(1)$

4. $602{,}920 = 6(100{,}000) + 2(1000) + 9(100) + 2(10)$

5. $8.25 = 8(1) + 2(0.1) + 5(0.01)$

6. $12.044 = 1(10) + 2(1) + 4(0.01) + 4(0.001)$

7. 4.4 m

8. 30 m

9. 1.25 m

10. 0.022 m

11. $\frac{54}{100} = \frac{27}{50}$

12. $\frac{95}{1000} = \frac{19}{200}$

13. $\frac{87}{100}$

14. $\frac{12}{100} = \frac{3}{25}$

15. \$8.75; \$26.24

Answers for Lesson 5.3, pages 233–235

Ongoing Assessment

1. 46   **2.** 52   **3.** 58

Practice and Problem Solving

1.

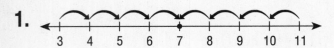

The average or mean is 7.

2. 8; 2; 5

3. 33

4. 41

5. 6.2

6. 114

7. 8

8. 9

9. 6

10. 60

11. 36

12. 104

13. 54

14. 74

15. 93

16. 262

17. 190

18. 435

19. 30

20. 27

21. *Sample answer:* Any set of 5 numbers that add to 50.

22. Average is 39 miles.

23. 132; 153

24. C

25. B

26. *Sample answer:* The mean of the survey is less than the mean of the 5 numbers. So members of our class have a greater tendency to read for pleasure.

Answers for Lesson 5.4, pages 237–240

Ongoing Assessment

1. Range: $12; mean: $8; median: $7; mode: $6

2. *Sample answer:* Half the employees earn more than the median and half earn less. The mode is the most commonly earned wage; mode; about half of the employees earn $6 per hour.

Practice and Problem Solving

1. Range: 142; median: 50; mode: 70; mean: 55.8

2. True

3. False; data has no mode.

4. False; median is mean of two middle numbers or 6.5.

5. Median: 46.5; mode: 45

6. Median: 134; mode: 122

7. Median: 12; modes: 11, 12

8. C

9. B

10. A

11. Range: 251; median: 143; mode: 111

12. *Sample answer:* Half of the songs on the CD are longer than the median and half are shorter. The mode tells you what is the most common song length.

13. *Sample answer:* The median; because it is the "middle" length.

14. Range: 57; mean: 41; median: 41; modes: 26, 39, 41, 46, 47

15. 23, 25, 26, 28, 28

16. Mean: 13.5; median: 12; mode: 12; the age of the adult, the chorus director, makes the mean larger.

(continued)

Answers for Lesson 5.4, pages 237–240 (cont.)

17. Mean: 26; median: 23.5; two modes, 20 and 40; *Sample answer:* The mode is not the best measure because the two modes are far apart.

18. B

19. B

20. B

21. Answers vary.

22. Answers vary.

Answers for Spiral Review, page 240

1. *Sample answer:*

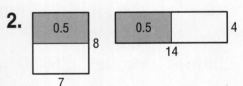

2.

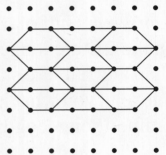

3.

4. 15; 10

5. 2

6. 3.45

7. 65

8.

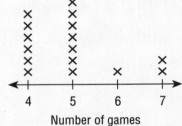

Number of games

Sample answer: Most years the Stanley Cup is decided in a 4 or 5 game series, and rarely in a 6 or 7 game series.

Answers for Mid-Chapter Assessment, page 241

1. A

2. C

3. B

4.

Number of Super Bowls

5. *Sample answer:* The most common number of Super Bowls won by a team is 1 and the range is 4.

6. 1; of teams that have won at least one Super Bowl, more have won only 1 than 2, 3, 4, or 5 games.

7.
```
0 | 1 3 4 4 4 5 7 9
1 | 0 0 0 2 3 4 6 7 7 7 7 8 9 9
2 | 1 2 3 5 9
3 | 2 5 6
4 | 5
```
Key: $4\,|\,5 = 45$

8. 49ers

9. Giants; The Giants only beat their opponent by 1 point.

10. 44

11. 28

12. 74

13. Mean: 15.875; median: 12; mode: 10
Sample answer: The median best describes the data because it is in the middle of the values.

Answers for Lesson 5.5, pages 243–245

Ongoing Assessment

1. *Sample answer:* A scale that increases by hundreds.

2.

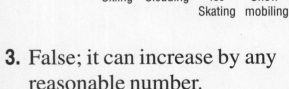

Practice and Problem Solving

1. *Sample answer:* Use a scale that increases by 20.

2.

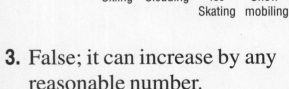

3. False; it can increase by any reasonable number.

4. Scale does not start at 0.

5. Bars are different widths.

6. Grid lines are not evenly spaced.

7. A

8. C

9. B

10. *Sample answer:* Include $5 increments.

11.

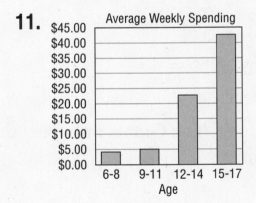

12.

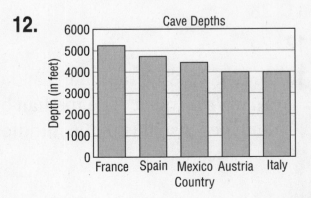

(continued)

13. *Sample answer:* Numbers on the scale are too large and too far apart for line plot.

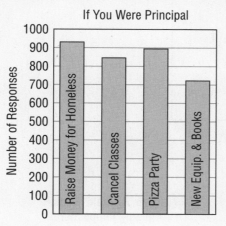

14. C

15. Answers vary.

16.

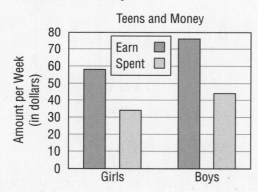

Answers for Lesson 5.6, pages 247–250

Practice and Problem Solving

1. Grid lines not evenly spaced.

2. Numbers do not start at 0.

3. Yes; the line slopes upward from the left to the right.

4. *Sample answer:* 14 million; the number continued to increase even faster.

5. *Sample answer:* 20

6. *Sample answer:* 30

7.

Fruit Juice Consumed in a Year

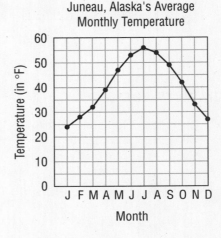

8.

Juneau, Alaska's Average Monthly Temperature

April and May

9. The amount of money spent on new cars increases and decreases while the money spent on used cars continually increases.

10. *Sample answer:* around $65 billion

11. *Sample answer:* If present trends continue, the line should eventually cross.

12. B   13. D

(continued)

Answers for Lesson 5.6, pages 247–250 (cont.)

14. a.

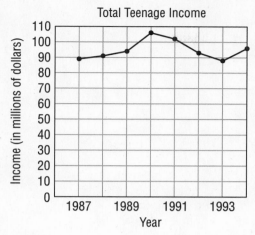

b. Answers vary.

15. a.

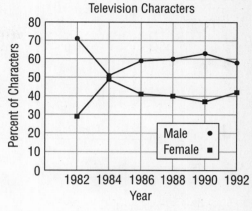

b. Answers vary.

Answers for Spiral Review, page 250

1. 12

2. 24

3. 18

4. 15

5. 34.5

6. 1.1

7. 3.8

8. 5.5

9. 2

10. 5

11. 27

12. 3

13. 14.32

14. 10.54

15. 8.77

16. 5.08

17. False; 0.048

18. True

19. True

20. False; 480

21.

0	1 2 3 5 6 6 8 9
1	1 3 4 4 5 8
2	0 2 7
3	1 8
4	0

Key: 3 | 1 = 31

Answers for Communicating About Mathematics, page 251

1. Yes; the percents add up to more than 100.

2. a. 13,050,000

    b. 7,540,000

3.

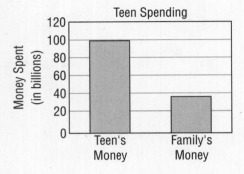

Answers vary.

4.

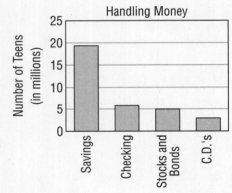

Answers vary.

Answers for Lesson 5.7, pages 253–255

Ongoing Assessment

1. Yes, you can use a pictograph to represent the data.

2. *Sample answer:* any kind of data that change over time, such as the amount of time spent on homework each week

---

Practice and Problem Solving

1. Yes; unequal flower sizes.

2. No

3. Yes; no key is provided.

4. Bar graph; *sample answer:* number of feeding times per day

5. Line plot; *sample answer:* ages of the members of a youth basketball team

6. Line graph; *sample answer:* the price of a stock over a four year period

7. D

8. E

9. A

10. B

11. C

12.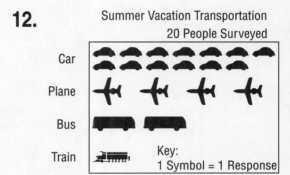

13.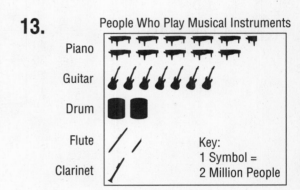

14. Answers vary; bar graph or pictograph.

15. A line plot; a stem-and-leaf plot would have only 2 stems.

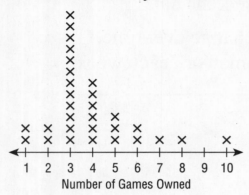

16. A line graph; a bar graph or pictograph is also suitable.

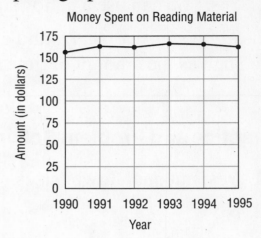

17.

4	0 4 5
5	4 6
6	4 7
7	4 9
8	3 5 7

Key: 4 | 0 = 40

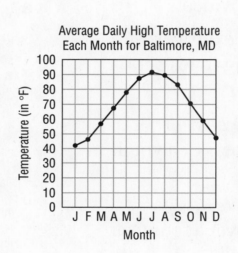

18. A

19. Answers vary.

Answers for Chapter Review, pages 257–259

1.

```
  ×
  ×    ×    ×
  ×    ×    ×    ×
<———————————————————>
  5    6    7    8
 Number of Letters in a Name
```

2. 3

3. 34

4.
3	5 5 5
4	0 3 4
5	1
6	9

Key: $3 \mid 5 = 35$

5. 35

6. 0.915

7. 0.995

8. There is no mode.

9.

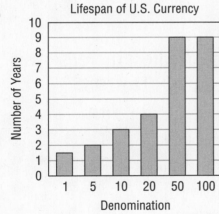

Lifespan of U.S. Currency

10.

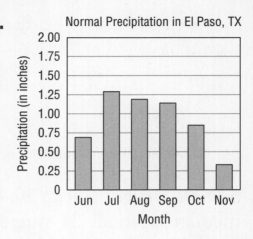

Normal Precipitation in El Paso, TX

11.

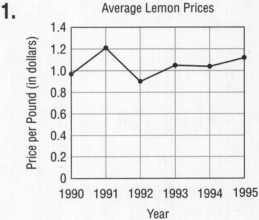

Average Lemon Prices

1991

12.

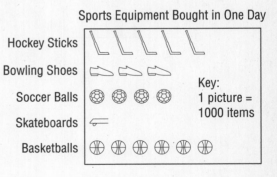

Sports Equipment Bought in One Day

Answers for Chapter Assessment, page 260

1.

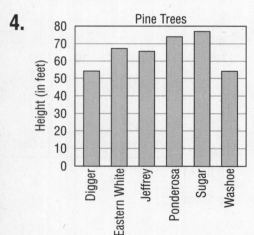

2. *Sample answer:* mean 30.42, median 31, mode 31, range $31 - 28 = 3$, longest 31, shortest 28.

3.

5	4 4
6	6 7
7	4 7

Key: $6 \mid 6 = 66$

4.

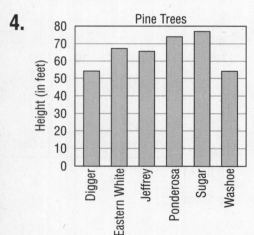

Pine Trees

5. 43

6. 75

7. Range: 20
Mean: 15.6
Median: 16
Mode: 16

8.

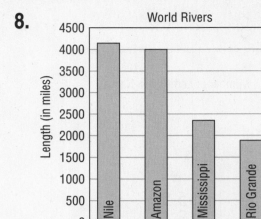

World Rivers

9.

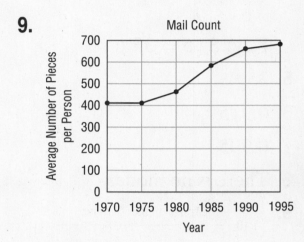

Mail Count

The greatest increase was from 1980 to 1985.

10.

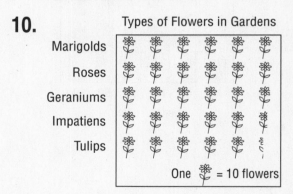

Types of Flowers in Gardens

One 🌼 = 10 flowers

Answers for Standardized Test Practice, page 261

1. D

2. D

3. C

4. C

5. B

6. A

Ongoing Assessment

1. $\frac{3}{5}$

2. The class divided into 3 equal groups

Practice and Problem Solving

1. No; all parts are not the same size.

2. Numerator; denominator

3. Mixed number

4. 12

5. C

6. A

7. B

8. *Sample answer:* when describing a child's age, when measuring something with a ruler, when weighing fruit on a scale at the supermarket

9. Yes; $\frac{2}{3}$

10. No; unequal sizes.

11. Yes; $\frac{4}{8}$

12. Yes; $\frac{3}{6}$

13. Yes; $\frac{2}{10}$

14. No; unequal sizes.

15.

16. a. 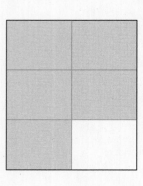   b.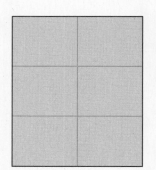

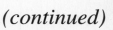

(continued)

Answers for Lesson 6.1, pages 269–271 (cont.)

17.

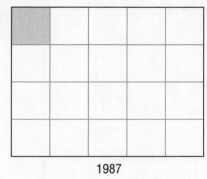

1987   1994

18. $\frac{2}{3}$; $\frac{3}{4}$

19. Second litter

20. *Sample answer:* $\frac{1}{7}$, $\frac{1}{9}$, $\frac{2}{10}$; $\frac{7}{8}$, $\frac{11}{12}$, $\frac{15}{16}$

21.

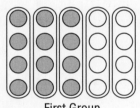

First Group   Second Group

Second group

22. $\frac{3}{4}$; it is 3 groups of 5, or 15; $\frac{3}{5}$ is 3 groups of 4, or 12.

23. D

24. C

(continued)

25. *Sample answer:*

Bedroom B $\frac{4}{25}$			Bedroom A $\frac{6}{25}$	
			Bathroom $\frac{2}{25}$	
	Living Room $\frac{9}{25}$		Kitchen $\frac{4}{25}$	

Ongoing Assessment

1. $\frac{9}{14}, \frac{9}{14}, \frac{9}{14}, \frac{9}{14}$ 2. Yes

Practice and Problem Solving

1. Divide each sandwich into 5 equal parts; 4 parts or $\frac{4}{5}$ of the sandwich.

2. $\frac{3}{2}$

3.  $\frac{7}{4}$ apples

4. *Sample answer:* comparing 2 numbers by division.

5.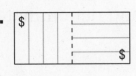

24 coins

6.

200 miles

7. $\frac{3}{5}$

8. $\frac{5}{3}$ or $1\frac{2}{3}$

9.

$\frac{1}{2}$

10.

$\frac{5}{7}$

(continued)

11.

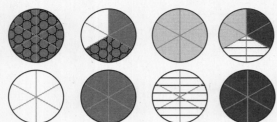

$1\frac{1}{3}$

12.

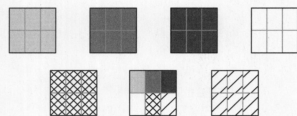

$1\frac{1}{6}$

13. *Sample answer:* the ratio of the distance from your town to each of two nearby cities

14. *Sample answer:* the ratio of the number of mystery books to the number of adventure books on your bookshelf

15. *Sample answer:* the ratio of the width to the length of your house

16. $\frac{7}{18}$

17. $\frac{12}{25}$

18. $\frac{12}{48}$ or $\frac{1}{4}$

19. $\frac{8}{12}$ or $\frac{2}{3}$

20. $\frac{16}{8}$ or $\frac{2}{1}$

21. $\frac{40}{41}$

22. A

23. Answers vary. Square rooms have ratios with the same numerator and denominator.

24. $\frac{216}{27}$ or $\frac{8}{1}$

Answers for Lesson 6.3, pages 279–281

Ongoing Assessment

1. Scale drawing: $\frac{4}{4}$; actual: $\frac{12}{12}$

2. $\frac{4}{4} = \frac{4 \cdot 3}{4 \cdot 3} = \frac{12}{12}$, the ratios are equivalent.

Practice and Problem Solving

1. $\frac{3}{5}$ or $\frac{6}{10}$

2.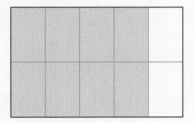

3.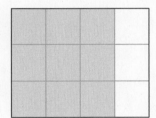

4. $\frac{1}{3}, \frac{2}{4}$; no

5. Yes; $\frac{1}{6} \cdot \frac{2}{2} = \frac{2}{12}$

6. No; $\frac{1}{2} \cdot \frac{4}{4} = \frac{4}{8}$ or $\frac{1}{2} \cdot \frac{3}{3} = \frac{3}{6}$

7. Yes; $\frac{5}{8} \cdot \frac{3}{3} = \frac{15}{24}$

8. No, $\frac{2}{5} \cdot \frac{2}{2} = \frac{4}{10}$

9. $\frac{2}{3} \cdot \frac{2}{2} = \frac{4}{6}$ or $\frac{2}{3} \cdot \frac{3}{3} = \frac{6}{9}$

10. B; *Sample answer:* $\frac{6}{18}$

11. C; *Sample answer:* $\frac{16}{28}$

12. D; *Sample answer:* $\frac{2}{3}$

13. A; *Sample answer:* $\frac{6}{8}$

14. 10   **16.** 9

15. 1   **17.** 42

18. *Sample answer:* $\frac{14}{16}, \frac{21}{24}, \frac{28}{32}$

19. *Sample answer:* $\frac{8}{22}, \frac{12}{33}, \frac{16}{44}$

20. *Sample answer:* $\frac{5}{6}, \frac{10}{12}, \frac{20}{24}$

21. *Sample answer:* $\frac{1}{9}, \frac{2}{18}, \frac{3}{27}$

22. False; 12

23. True

24. True

(continued)

Answers for Lesson 6.3, pages 279–281 (cont.)

25.

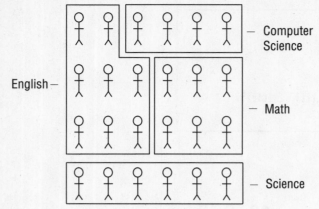

Science: 6; English: 8;
Computer Science: 4; Math: 6

26. $\frac{6}{24}$

27. 4 students

28. No; Ricardo walked at a rate of 4 miles per hour and Suzy walked at a rate of 3 miles per hour.

29. Yes; $\frac{6}{36} = \frac{1 \cdot 6}{6 \cdot 6} = \frac{1}{6} \cdot \frac{5}{5} = \frac{5}{30}$

30. A

31. C

32. Answers vary.

Answers for Lesson 6.4, pages 283–285

Ongoing Assessment

1. 12   **2.** 3   **3.** Answers vary.

Practice and Problem Solving

1. C

2. A

3. B

4. D

5. $\frac{9}{21}, \frac{3}{7}$ and $\frac{6}{14}; \frac{3}{7}$

6. $\frac{6}{18} = \frac{1}{3}$

7.

12

8. Answers vary.

9. $\frac{4}{16}; \frac{1}{4}$

10. $\frac{12}{28}; \frac{3}{7}$

11. $\frac{3}{8}$

12. $\frac{1}{6}$

13. Not possible

14. $\frac{4}{3}$

15. 1

16. $\frac{2}{5}$

17. 7

18. $\frac{8}{9}$

19. $\frac{5}{8}$

20. $\frac{3}{7}$

21. Not possible

22. $\frac{5}{8}$

23. Not possible

24. False; fractions are not equivalent.

25. False; fractions are not equivalent.

26. True; $\frac{2}{7} \cdot \frac{5}{5} = \frac{10}{35}$

27. 30

28. 7

29. 8

30. 11

31. 12

32. 63

33. $\frac{8}{28} = \frac{x}{7}$; 2 feet

(continued)

Answers for Lesson 6.4, pages 283–285 (cont.)

34. $\frac{9}{16} = \frac{18}{x}$; 32 cm

35. No; $\frac{100 \text{ mi}}{5 \text{ gal}} = \frac{20 \text{ mi}}{1 \text{ gal}}$ and $\frac{150 \text{ mi}}{8 \text{ gal}} = \frac{75 \text{ mi}}{4 \text{ gal}}$

36. $31; 155 \div 5 = 31$

37. D

38. B

39. 6 rolls; answers vary.

Answers for Spiral Review, page 286

1.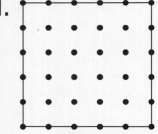

2.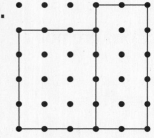

3. 20

4. 12.8

5. 1.35

6. $\frac{1}{2}$

7. $\frac{2}{3}$

8. $\frac{3}{5}$

9. $\frac{2}{3}$

10. 0.2

11. 0.49

12. 0.221

13. 0.7

Answers for Mid-Chapter Assessment, page 287

1. A

2. C

3. D

4. B

5.

$\frac{2}{3}$

6.

$\frac{8}{5}$

7. $\frac{6}{10}$ or $\frac{3}{5}$

8. $\frac{3}{5}$

9. $\frac{9}{15}$ or $\frac{3}{5}$

10. Yes, all ratios are equal to $\frac{3}{5}$.

11. Ratio; *sample answer:* the ratio of the width to the length of a patio

12. Rate; *sample answer:* your driving speed on a local road

13. Ratio; *sample answer:* the ratio of horses in stable A to horses in stable B

14. $\frac{5}{28}$

15. $\frac{5}{7}$

16. $\frac{1}{3}$

17. 8 feet

18. 1

19. 50

20. 45

Answers for Lesson 6.5, pages 291–294

Practice and Problem Solving

1. 1. Draw a model for the fractions.

   2. Write the fractions as decimals.

   3. Rewrite the fractions as equivalent fractions with the same denominator.

   Answers vary.

2. $\frac{1}{4}$ and $\frac{2}{5}$; $\frac{2}{5}$ is greater.

3.

   $\frac{1}{5} > \frac{1}{6}$

   $\frac{4}{5} > \frac{4}{6}$ because the fractions have the same numerator and fifths are greater than sixths.

4. $\frac{4}{9}$ is less than $\frac{1}{2}$ and $\frac{5}{9}$ is greater than $\frac{1}{2}$; therefore, $\frac{5}{9}$ is greater than $\frac{4}{9}$.

5. $\frac{1}{3}$ is less than $\frac{1}{2}$ and $\frac{3}{4}$ is greater than $\frac{1}{2}$; therefore, $\frac{3}{4}$ is greater than $\frac{1}{3}$.

6. $\frac{2}{3}$ is greater than $\frac{1}{2}$ and $\frac{3}{7}$ is less than $\frac{1}{2}$; therefore, $\frac{2}{3}$ is greater than $\frac{3}{7}$.

(continued)

Answers for Lesson 6.5, pages 291–294 (cont.)

7. $\frac{5}{6}$ and $\frac{4}{5}$; $\frac{5}{6}$ is greater.

8. $\frac{1}{3}$ and $\frac{1}{2}$; $\frac{1}{2}$ is greater.

9. $\frac{2}{4}$ equals $\frac{1}{2}$ and $\frac{3}{4}$ is greater than $\frac{1}{2}$; therefore, $\frac{3}{4}$ is greater than $\frac{2}{4}$.

10. $\frac{3}{5}$ is greater than $\frac{1}{2}$ and $\frac{3}{6}$ equals $\frac{1}{2}$; therefore, $\frac{3}{5}$ is greater than $\frac{3}{6}$.

11. $\frac{4}{6}$ is greater than $\frac{1}{2}$ and $\frac{3}{8}$ is less than $\frac{1}{2}$; therefore, $\frac{4}{6}$ is greater than $\frac{3}{8}$.

12. $\frac{5}{9}$ is greater than $\frac{1}{2}$ and $\frac{6}{13}$ is less than $\frac{1}{2}$; therefore, $\frac{5}{9}$ is greater than $\frac{6}{13}$.

13.

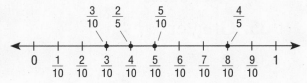

$$\frac{3}{10}, \frac{2}{5}, \frac{5}{10}, \frac{4}{5}$$

14.

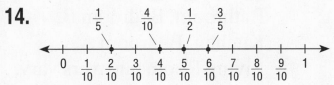

$$\frac{1}{5}, \frac{4}{10}, \frac{1}{2}, \frac{3}{5}$$

15.

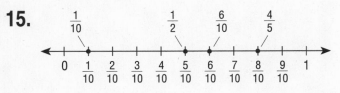

$$\frac{1}{10}, \frac{1}{2}, \frac{6}{10}, \frac{4}{5}$$

(continued)

16. $<$

17. $>$

18. $<$

19. $>$

20. Sample answer: $\frac{1}{4}$

21. Sample answer: $\frac{8}{9}$

22. Sample answer: $\frac{7}{8}$

23. Sample answer: $\frac{1}{2}$

24. Gina; $\frac{4}{5} > \frac{3}{4}$

25. Sample answer: $\frac{1}{4}$

26. Sample answer: $\frac{1}{2}$

27. Sample answer: $\frac{2}{5}$

28. $\frac{7}{8}$; $\frac{7}{8}$ is greater than $\frac{7}{9}$, $\frac{7}{10}$, and $\frac{7}{11}$.

29. $\frac{1}{7}$; $\frac{1}{7}$ is less than $\frac{1}{4}$, $\frac{1}{5}$, and $\frac{1}{6}$.

30. $\frac{4}{6}$

31. $\frac{3}{4}$

32. $\frac{7}{12}$

33. $\frac{7}{12}$, $\frac{4}{6}$, $\frac{3}{4}$

34. **a.** $\frac{52}{28}$ or $\frac{13}{7}$

　　b. $\frac{52}{24}$ or $\frac{13}{6}$

　　Gear set **a.**

35. Greater

36. D

37. A

38. $\frac{2}{25}$, $\frac{4}{25}$, $\frac{4}{25}$, $\frac{6}{25}$, $\frac{9}{25}$
Bathroom, Bedroom B, Kitchen, Bedroom A, Living Room; answers vary.

Answers for Spiral Review, page 294

1. 24

2. 3

3. 1

4. 7

5. 121

6. 11.09

7. 58.56

8. $\frac{48}{100}$; $\frac{12}{25}$

9. $\frac{6}{10}$; $\frac{3}{5}$

10. $\frac{32}{100}$; $\frac{8}{25}$

11. $\frac{150}{100}$; $\frac{3}{2}$ or $1\frac{1}{2}$

12. 2.02, 2.12, 2.19, 2.2, 2.3

13. 8.3, 8.32, 8.35, 8.45, 8.53

14. 0.009, 0.05, 0.09, 0.19, 0.6

15. 2.01, 2.015, 2.05, 2.105, 2.15

Answers for Lesson 6.6, pages 297–299

Ongoing Assessment

1. *Sample answer:* five $\frac{1}{2}$ cup measures

2. *Sample answer:* five $\frac{1}{4}$ cup measures

3. *Sample answer:* three $\frac{1}{4}$ cup measures

Practice and Problem Solving

1. It is equal to or greater than one; a proper fraction is less than 1.

2. $3\frac{1}{2}$; there are 3 whole parts and $\frac{1}{2}$ of another.

3. $\frac{7}{2}$

4. 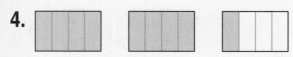 $\frac{9}{4}$

   1. Draw the model.
   2. Divide the whole parts into fourths.
   3. Add up the fourths.

5. $5\frac{2}{3}$

6. $\frac{19}{4}$

7. Always

8. Never

9. Sometimes

10. $1\frac{2}{5}$, $\frac{7}{5}$

11. $2\frac{4}{6}$, $\frac{16}{6}$

12. B

13. D

14. A

15. C

16.

   $1\frac{2}{5}$

17.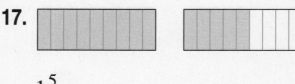

   $1\frac{5}{9}$

18.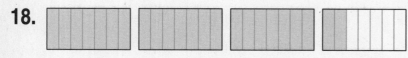

$3\frac{2}{7}$

(continued)

Answers for Lesson 6.6, pages 297–299 (cont.)

19.

$3\frac{1}{2}$

20.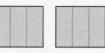

$5\frac{1}{3}$

21.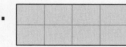

$1\frac{3}{8}$

22.

$3\frac{3}{4}$

23.

$4\frac{5}{6}$

24.

$\frac{5}{2}$

25.

$\frac{7}{4}$

26.

$\frac{13}{5}$

27.

$\frac{11}{3}$

(continued)

Answers for Lesson 6.6, pages 297–299 (cont.)

28.

$\frac{11}{7}$

29.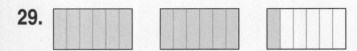

$\frac{13}{6}$

30.

$\frac{13}{4}$

31.

$\frac{23}{6}$

32. $\frac{9}{2}$ hours; $4\frac{1}{2}$ hours; answers vary.

33.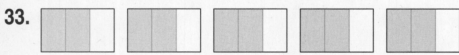

$\frac{10}{3}$ or $3\frac{1}{3}$

34. 17; $2\frac{5}{6}$ equals $\frac{17}{6}$.

35. B

36. C

37. Kitchen: 5 boxes; Bedroom B: 5 boxes; Bedroom A: $7\frac{1}{2}$ boxes; Living room: $11\frac{1}{4}$ boxes; answers vary.

Answers for Spiral Review, page 300

1. $30.00

2. 4.35 mm

3. 1.4 inches

4. February 3, 1991

5. 7¢

6.

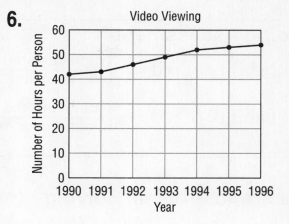

Sample answer: The number of hours spent per person watching videos increased steadily from 1990 to 1996.

Answers for Communicating About Mathematics, page 301

1. $\frac{72}{1}$

2. $\frac{1}{8}$

3. $\frac{1}{216}$

Ongoing Assessment

1. Probability of red $= \dfrac{\text{Number of red regions}}{\text{Total number of regions}} = \dfrac{6}{12} = \dfrac{1}{2}$

2. Probability of red $= \dfrac{\text{Number of red regions}}{\text{Total number of regions}} = \dfrac{4}{12} = \dfrac{1}{3}$

Practice and Problem Solving

1. $\dfrac{3}{10}$

2. $\dfrac{3}{10}$

3. $\dfrac{1}{2}$

4. $\dfrac{1}{2}$

5. Yes; Probability of even $+$ Probability of odd $= \dfrac{1}{2} + \dfrac{1}{2} = 1$

6. B

7. C

8. A

9. Answers vary.

10. Answers vary.

11. $\dfrac{1}{3}$

12. $\dfrac{5}{9}$

13. $\dfrac{3}{10}$

14. $\dfrac{5}{8}$

15. B

16. A

17. C

18. a. 0.29

    b. 0.05

19. $\dfrac{1}{4}$; 0.25

20. Answers vary.

21. $\dfrac{1}{2}$

22. $\dfrac{3}{4}$

23. C

24. A

25. 10

26. 20

Answers for Chapter Review, pages 307–309

1. $\frac{19}{8}$; $2\frac{3}{8}$

2. Numerator, denominator, mixed number

3. $\frac{3}{7}$

4. $\frac{12}{18}$ or $\frac{2}{3}$

5. 4

6. $\frac{10}{3}$ or $3\frac{1}{3}$

7. $\frac{5}{4}$ or $1\frac{1}{4}$

8. $\frac{3}{4}$

9. *Sample answer:* $\frac{12}{14}$, $\frac{18}{21}$, $\frac{24}{28}$

10. $\frac{28}{48}$ or $\frac{7}{12}$

11. $\frac{1}{3}$ ft

12. 7

13. $.36

14. $\frac{31}{32}$

15. $\frac{1}{2}$, $\frac{2}{3}$, $\frac{5}{6}$

16. $2\frac{5}{8}$, $\frac{21}{8}$

17.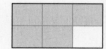

    $\frac{11}{6}$

18. $\frac{7}{4}$; 7

19. $\frac{8}{16}$ or $\frac{1}{2}$

20. 0

21. 1

22. $\frac{1}{2}$

Answers for Chapter Assessment, page 310

1. *Sample answer:* $\frac{1}{2}, \frac{3}{6}, \frac{6}{12}$

2. *Sample answer:* $\frac{1}{4}, \frac{2}{8}, \frac{4}{16}$

3. *Sample answer:* $\frac{2}{3}, \frac{8}{12}, \frac{16}{24}$

4. $\frac{5}{9} = \frac{15}{18}$; no

5. $\frac{24}{28} = \frac{6}{7}$; yes

6. $\frac{1}{2}$

7. $\frac{4}{5}$

8. $\frac{7}{10}$

9. $\frac{2}{9}$

10. False; 18

11. True

12. False; 4

13. $>$

14. $<$

15. $>$

16. $<$

17. $5\frac{2}{5}$

18. $\frac{19}{8}$

19.

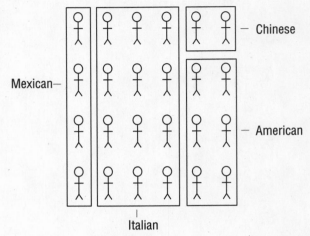

Mexican: 4, Italian: 12, Chinese: 2, American: 6

20. Likely to occur

21. Must occur

22. Cannot occur

23. Not likely to occur

Answers for Standardized Test Practice, page 311

1. C

2. B

3. C

4. A

5. D

6. C

7. B

8. D

9. C

10. A

Answers for Cumulative Review, pages 312 and 313

1. 12

2. 11

3. 5

4. 35

5. 3

6. 100

7. 3

8. 8

9. 16

10. 9050

11. 27

12. 48

13. 1.39

14. 0.9 or $\frac{9}{10}$

15. $\frac{2}{3}$

16. 2800

17. 70

18. 92

19. 48

20. 15

21. 14

22. 3.02, 3.12, 3.19, 3.2, 3.22

23. 0.01, 0.011, 0.02, 0.1, 0.11

24. $\frac{3}{8}, \frac{4}{8}, \frac{3}{5}, \frac{3}{4}$

25. $\frac{1}{2}, \frac{4}{7}, \frac{2}{3}, \frac{4}{5}$

26. 950

27. 1600

28. 84,000

29. 15

30. 0.5

31. 7.85

32. 8.5

33. 8.5

34. 2.44

35. Range: 6
    Median: 14
    Mode: 14
    Mean: 14

36. Range: 6
    Median: 39
    Mode: 39
    Mean: 40

37. Answers vary.

38. 24

39.

2	8
3	4
4	0 0 5 5
5	0 0 5
6	0 5 5
7	0 0 0 5 5 5 5
8	0 0 0 0 5

Key: 4 | 0 = 40

(continued)

40. 75 and 80 lb

41. 28 lb

42.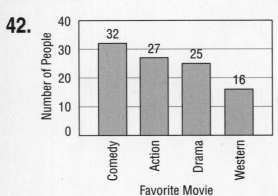

43. 27%

44. Drama

45. *Sample answer:* line graph; it should enable you to see the changes in the number of cellular phones over the years.

46. 1991

47. 12 calls

Answers for Lesson 7.1, pages 319–321

Ongoing Assessment

1. a. 71 inches   **b.** 72 inches   **c.** 6 feet 2 inches

2. 74 inches

Practice and Problem Solving

1. $\frac{3}{4}$ in.

2. $\frac{7}{8}$ in.

3. $\frac{1}{8}, \frac{2}{8}, \frac{3}{8}, \frac{4}{8}, \frac{5}{8}, \frac{6}{8}, \frac{7}{8}, \frac{8}{8}$; number increases by $\frac{1}{8}$.

4. $8\frac{3}{8}$ in. by $10\frac{3}{4}$ in.; $38\frac{1}{4}$ in.

5. 2

6. 30

7. $2\frac{5}{8}$ in.; C

8. $3\frac{3}{4}$ in.; D

9. $4\frac{1}{2}$ in.; E

10. $1\frac{7}{8}$ in.; B

11. $1\frac{1}{8}$ in.; A

12. $1\frac{1}{2}$ in.

13. $\frac{7}{8}$ in.

14. $1\frac{3}{4}$ in.

15. *Sample answer:* a kitchen table

16. *Sample answer:* a football field

17. *Sample answer:* a desk

18. *Sample answer:* a house

19. 6′3″

20. 5 feet 11 inches

21. $4'5\frac{1}{2}''$

22. $5'7\frac{3}{4}''$

23. 3

24. 5

25. 180

26. 9

27. 18

28. 3

29. 23 yd

30. $12\frac{1}{2}$ ft

31. $7\frac{3}{8}$ in.

32. $3\frac{1}{6}$ yds long and $\frac{5}{6}$ yd wide

33. D

34. a. $3\frac{7}{8}$ in.

     b. $3\frac{7}{8}$ miles

Ongoing Assessment

1. $\frac{9}{24}, \frac{20}{24}, \frac{14}{24}$

   $\frac{3}{8} = \frac{3 \cdot 3}{8 \cdot 3} = \frac{9}{24}; \frac{5}{6} = \frac{5 \cdot 4}{6 \cdot 4} = \frac{20}{24}; \frac{7}{12} = \frac{7 \cdot 2}{12 \cdot 2} = \frac{14}{24}$

2. Because the denominators are the same, the greater fraction is the one with the greater numerator.

Practice and Problem Solving

1. C; it shows 3 out of 12 parts, or $\frac{1}{4}$.

2. True; $3 \cdot 10 = 30, 5 \cdot 6 = 30, 3 \cdot 15 = 45,$ $5 \cdot 9 = 45$

3. False; 15 is a common multiple of 3 and 5.

4. True; the least common multiple of 3 and 5 is 15.

5. False; there may be a common multiple of two numbers that is less than their product.

6. $\frac{2}{5}$; *Sample answer:* rewrite them with a common denominator.

7. 5, 10, 15, 20, 25, 30, 35, <u>40</u>, 45, 50;
   8, 16, 24, 32, <u>40</u>, 48, 56, 64, 72, 80;
   least common multiple: 40

8. 10, <u>20</u>, 30, 40, 50, 60, 70, 80, 90, 100;
   4, 8, 12, 16, <u>20</u>, 24, 28, 32, 36, 40;
   least common multiple: 20

9. 5, 10, 15, 20, 25, <u>30</u>, 35, 40, 45, 50;
   6, 12, 18, 24, <u>30</u>, 36, 42, 48, 54, 60;
   least common multiple: 30

(continued)

Answers for Lesson 7.2, pages 323–326 (cont.)

10. 12, 24, 36, 48, <u>60</u>, 72, 84, 96, 108, 120;
10, 20, 30, 40, 50, <u>60</u>, 70, 80, 90, 100;
least common multiple: 60

11. *Sample answer:*

 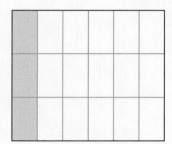

12. *Sample answer:*

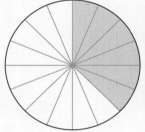 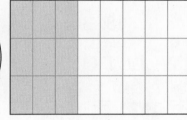

13. *Sample answer:*

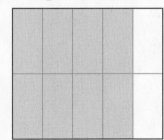 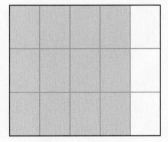

(continued)

14. *Sample answer:*

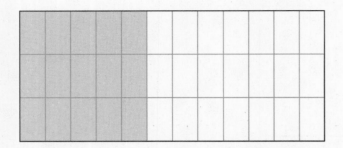

15. $12; \frac{4}{12}, \frac{11}{12}$

16. $24; \frac{16}{24}, \frac{21}{24}$

17. $30; \frac{5}{30}, \frac{21}{30}$

18. $30; \frac{6}{30}, \frac{15}{30}$

19. $\frac{2}{24}, \frac{4}{24}, \frac{9}{24}, \frac{10}{24}, \frac{16}{24}, \frac{20}{24}, \frac{21}{24}, \frac{22}{24}$; WELL DONE

20. Distance: $\frac{5}{8} = \frac{5 \cdot 3}{8 \cdot 3} = \frac{15}{24}, \frac{7}{12} = \frac{7 \cdot 2}{12 \cdot 2} = \frac{14}{24}$, you walked farther.

Time: $\frac{3}{5} = \frac{3 \cdot 3}{5 \cdot 3} = \frac{9}{15}; \frac{2}{3} = \frac{2 \cdot 5}{3 \cdot 5} = \frac{10}{15}$, your friend walked longer.

Speed: Since you walked farther in less time, you walked faster.

21. $\frac{2}{5}, \frac{3}{10}, \frac{3}{10}$

22. Saw, Cow, See, One, But, can, you, See, One; $\frac{9}{24}$ or $\frac{3}{8}$

23. $\frac{3}{12}$ or $\frac{1}{4}$

24. *The Purple Cow*

25. B

26. A

27. No

Passport to Mathematics Book 1

Answers for Spiral Review, page 326

1. **a.** $3 \times .75 + 2 \times .50 + 4 \times .25$
   b. $4.25

2. $>$

3. $=$

4. $=$

5. $<$

6. $\begin{array}{r} 4.50 \\ + \ 3.35 \\ \hline 7.85 \end{array}$

7. $\begin{array}{r} 16.00 \\ - \ \ 3.54 \\ \hline 12.46 \end{array}$

8. $\begin{array}{r} 12.92 \\ + \ \ 3.56 \\ \hline 16.48 \end{array}$

9. $\begin{array}{r} 10.66 \\ - \ \ 8.98 \\ \hline 1.68 \end{array}$

10. 100

11. 1000

12. 32

13. 10,000

14.

Mode is 17, range is 9; answers vary.

15. 12

16. 8 yd^2

Answers for Lesson 7.3, pages 331–333

Ongoing Assessment

1. $\dfrac{4}{5} + \dfrac{2}{3} = \dfrac{4 \cdot 3}{5 \cdot 3} + \dfrac{2 \cdot 5}{3 \cdot 5}$

   $= \dfrac{12}{15} + \dfrac{10}{15}$

   $= \dfrac{12 + 10}{15}$

   $= \dfrac{22}{15}$

2. $\dfrac{7}{8} - \dfrac{1}{2} = \dfrac{7}{8} - \dfrac{1 \cdot 4}{2 \cdot 4}$

   $= \dfrac{7}{8} - \dfrac{4}{8}$

   $= \dfrac{7 - 4}{8}$

   $= \dfrac{3}{8}$

3. $\dfrac{1}{3} + \dfrac{1}{2} + \dfrac{1}{6} = \dfrac{1 \cdot 2}{3 \cdot 2} + \dfrac{1 \cdot 3}{2 \cdot 3} + \dfrac{1}{6}$

   $= \dfrac{2}{6} + \dfrac{3}{6} + \dfrac{1}{6}$

   $= \dfrac{2 + 3 + 1}{6}$

   $= \dfrac{6}{6}$

   $= 1$

Practice and Problem Solving

1. Always; $\dfrac{3}{5} - \dfrac{1}{5} = \dfrac{2}{5}$; $\dfrac{4}{6} - \dfrac{2}{6} = \dfrac{2}{6}$

2. Sometimes; $\dfrac{1}{7} + \dfrac{2}{7} + \dfrac{3}{7} = \dfrac{6}{7}$; $\dfrac{1}{4} + \dfrac{2}{4} + \dfrac{3}{4} = \dfrac{6}{4} = 1\dfrac{2}{4}$

3. Sometimes; least common denominator of $\dfrac{1}{5}$ and $\dfrac{1}{3}$ is 15, least common denominator of $\dfrac{1}{6}$ and $\dfrac{1}{8}$ is 24.

(continued)

4. If two fractions have a common denominator, add the numerators and keep the denominator.

$$\frac{1}{8} + \frac{5}{8} = \frac{6}{8}$$

If two fractions have different denominators, first rewrite them with a common denominator, then proceed with your addition or subtraction.

$$\frac{1}{3} + \frac{1}{5} = \frac{5}{15} + \frac{3}{15} = \frac{8}{15}$$

5. a. Rewrite numerator as well as denominator.

$$\frac{1}{3} + \frac{3}{5} = \frac{1 \cdot 5}{3 \cdot 5} + \frac{3 \cdot 3}{5 \cdot 3} = \frac{5}{15} + \frac{9}{15} = \frac{5 + 9}{15} = \frac{14}{15}$$

b. Keep the same denominator.

$$\frac{2}{3} + \frac{1}{6} = \frac{4}{6} + \frac{1}{6} = \frac{5}{6}$$

6.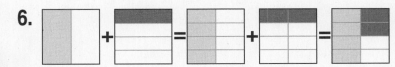

$$\frac{3}{4}$$

7.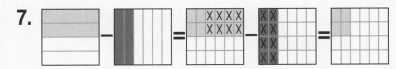

$$\frac{1}{6}$$

8. $1\frac{1}{3}$

9. $\frac{1}{10}$

10. $\frac{1}{2}$

11. $1\frac{3}{5}$

12. $\frac{9}{14}$

13. $\frac{8}{21}$

14. $\frac{4}{7}$

15. $\frac{3}{10}$

(continued)

Answers for Lesson 7.3, pages 331–333 (cont.)

16. Answers vary; $\frac{6}{3}$, $\frac{4}{3}$

17. Answers vary; $\frac{1}{8}$, $\frac{1}{8}$

18. $\frac{3}{8}$

19. $\frac{1}{6}$

20. $1\frac{1}{7}$ ft

21. $2\frac{1}{12}$ yd

22. $\frac{1}{3}$ in.

23. $\frac{3}{4}$; no

24. $\frac{15}{16}$; no

25. 1; yes

26. C

27. a. You, $\frac{1}{15}$

    b. 160

Answers for Lesson 7.4, pages 337–339

Ongoing Assessment

1. $3\frac{3}{4} + 2\frac{3}{4} = 5\frac{6}{4}$

    $\phantom{3\frac{3}{4} + 2\frac{3}{4}} = 5 + \frac{4}{4} + \frac{2}{4}$

    $\phantom{3\frac{3}{4} + 2\frac{3}{4}} = 5 + 1 + \frac{2}{4}$

    $\phantom{3\frac{3}{4} + 2\frac{3}{4}} = 6 + \frac{2}{4}$

    $\phantom{3\frac{3}{4} + 2\frac{3}{4}} = 6\frac{2}{4}$

    $\phantom{3\frac{3}{4} + 2\frac{3}{4}} = 6\frac{1}{2}$

2. $6\frac{5}{6} - 4\frac{1}{2} = 6\frac{5}{6} - 4\frac{3}{6}$

    $\phantom{6\frac{5}{6} - 4\frac{1}{2}} = 2\frac{2}{6}$

    $\phantom{6\frac{5}{6} - 4\frac{1}{2}} = 2\frac{1}{3}$

Practice and Problem Solving

1. *Sample answer:*

    Sum: place ruler with $5\frac{5}{8}$ in. mark at the beginning of $3\frac{1}{4}$ in. line segment. Read marking at the end of the segment. $8\frac{7}{8}$ in.

    Difference: measure and mark $3\frac{1}{4}$ in. along $5\frac{5}{8}$ in. segment. Measure remaining part of segment. $2\frac{3}{8}$ in.

2. $2\frac{5}{7} + 6\frac{4}{7} = 8\frac{9}{7}$ Add fractions and whole numbers.

    $\phantom{2\frac{5}{7} + 6\frac{4}{7}} = 8 + \frac{7}{7} + \frac{2}{7}$ Simplify mixed number.

    $\phantom{2\frac{5}{7} + 6\frac{4}{7}} = 9\frac{2}{7}$

(continued)

Answers for Lesson 7.4, pages 337–339 (cont.)

3. $4\frac{5}{6} - 2\frac{1}{3} = 4\frac{5}{6} - 2\frac{2}{6}$ Rewrite with common denominator.

$\qquad\qquad = 2\frac{3}{6}$ Subtract fractions and whole numbers.

$\qquad\qquad = 2\frac{1}{2}$ Simplify mixed number.

4. B

5. C

6. D

7. A

8. $2\frac{3}{5} + 5\frac{1}{4} = 7\frac{17}{20}$

9. $6\frac{8}{9} - 2\frac{4}{9} = 4\frac{4}{9}$

10. $7\frac{3}{6} - 4\frac{1}{6} = 3\frac{1}{3}$

11. $3\frac{6}{8} + 1\frac{1}{2} = 5\frac{1}{4}$

12. $12\frac{4}{5}$

13. $3\frac{4}{8}$ or $3\frac{1}{2}$

14. $7\frac{4}{9}$

15. $11\frac{2}{10}$ or $11\frac{1}{5}$

16. $8\frac{5}{12}$

17. $4\frac{1}{15}$

18. $5\frac{3}{12}$ or $5\frac{1}{4}$

19. $9\frac{19}{24}$

20. Your friend; $\frac{1}{30}$ of a bottle

21. 6

22. $9\frac{1}{3}$

23. $1\frac{2}{8}$ or $1\frac{1}{4}$

24. $\frac{1}{4}$

25. $\frac{1}{5}$

26. $2\frac{1}{2}$

27. $1\frac{6}{8}$ or $1\frac{3}{4}$, $1\frac{5}{8}$, $1\frac{4}{8}$ or $1\frac{1}{2}$; each answer decreases by $\frac{1}{8}$.

28. $8\frac{4}{6}$ or $8\frac{2}{3}$, $8\frac{3}{6}$ or $8\frac{1}{2}$, $8\frac{2}{6}$ or $8\frac{1}{3}$; each answer decreases by $\frac{1}{6}$.

29. $8\frac{1}{5}$, $8\frac{2}{5}$, $8\frac{3}{5}$; each answer increases by $\frac{1}{5}$.

30. 4.5 or $4\frac{1}{2}$

31. $3\frac{3}{5}$ and $2\frac{1}{5}$

32. $4\frac{1}{3}$ ft

33. C

34. a. $5\frac{3}{4}$ c

     b. 2 c

     c. $1\frac{1}{12}$ c

     d. $4\frac{1}{2}$ t

Answers for Spiral Review, page 340

1. 120 ways
2. A rectangle divided into 10 equal areas.
3. 100 triangles
4. 56
5. 106
6. 325
7. 86
8. $\frac{1}{9}$

9. $\frac{1}{2}$
10. 5
11. $\frac{1}{5}$
12. $\frac{14}{5}$
13. $\frac{37}{9}$
14. $\frac{47}{12}$
15. $\frac{67}{10}$

Answers for Mid-Chapter Assessment, page 341

1. $1\frac{7}{8}$ in.; $\frac{15}{8}$ in.
2. $2\frac{1}{8}$ in.; $\frac{17}{8}$ in.
3. 76 in.
4. No
5. Yes
6. No
7. Yes
8. E
9. C
10. D
11. A
12. F
13. B

14. 1
15. $\frac{4}{15}$
16. $\frac{7}{18}$
17. $\frac{11}{12}$
18. 1
19. $\frac{9}{24}$ or $\frac{3}{8}$
20. 6
21. $7\frac{1}{2}$
22. $4\frac{3}{5}$
23. Less; she lost $\frac{1}{5} + \frac{1}{4} = \frac{9}{20}$ which is less than $\frac{10}{20}$.

Answers for Lesson 7.5, pages 343–345

Practice and Problem Solving

1. B

2. C

3. A

4. $5.00 - 1.35 = 3.65$;
   $4\frac{100}{100} - 1\frac{35}{100} = 3\frac{65}{100}$;
   answers vary.

5. $2\frac{3}{4}$ yd^2

6. $1\frac{1}{2}$ yd^2

7. 8

8. 7

9. 5

10. 8

11. $=$

12. $>$

13. $<$

14. $=$

15. $14\frac{2}{3}$ yd

16. $1\frac{7}{8}$

17. $2\frac{5}{12}$

18. $2\frac{1}{2}$

19. $1\frac{4}{5}$

20. $\frac{3}{4}$

21. $1\frac{8}{9}$

22. $2\frac{1}{3}$

23. $2\frac{3}{5}$

24. $1\frac{2}{3}$

25. $2\frac{1}{3}$

26. $1\frac{2}{3}$

27. $3\frac{1}{3}$

28. $2\frac{3}{10}$ miles; $6.0 - 3\frac{7}{10} = 2\frac{3}{10}$
    or $6.0 - 3.7 = 2.3$

29. A

30. Music

31. Mouse

32. Blue

33. Answers vary.

Answers for Lesson 7.6, pages 349–351

Ongoing Assessment

1. $3\frac{1}{2} - 2\frac{5}{8} = 3\frac{4}{8} - 2\frac{5}{8}$

$\qquad\qquad = 2\frac{12}{8} - 2\frac{5}{8}$

$\qquad\qquad = \frac{7}{8}$

2. $5\frac{3}{8} - 2\frac{5}{6} = 5\frac{9}{24} - 2\frac{20}{24}$

$\qquad\qquad = 4\frac{33}{24} - 2\frac{20}{24}$

$\qquad\qquad = 2\frac{13}{24}$

Practice and Problem Solving

1. Rename; $\frac{2}{3}$ and $\frac{1}{4}$ have different denominators; $2\frac{5}{12}$.

2. Regroup; $\frac{1}{8}$ is smaller than $\frac{5}{8}$; $\frac{1}{2}$.

3. Rename; $\frac{7}{12}$ and $\frac{1}{3}$ have different denominators; $1\frac{1}{4}$.

4. *Sample answer:* $3\frac{2}{9} - 1\frac{5}{9}$

5. D, B, C, and A

6. D

7. C

8. B

9. A

10. $3\frac{21}{40}$

11. $2\frac{19}{24}$

12. $1\frac{1}{2}$

13. $2\frac{13}{24}$

14. $\frac{4}{9}$

15. $11\frac{7}{15}$

16. $2\frac{5}{16}$

17. $4\frac{5}{6}$

18. $2\frac{93}{100}$ mi

19. $1\frac{87}{100}$ mi

20. $\frac{17}{50}$ mi

(continued)

Answers for Lesson 7.6, pages 349–351 (cont.)

21. $\frac{18}{25}$ mi

22. $4\frac{3}{4}$ in.

23. $2\frac{1}{2}$ in.

24.

25. D

26. $\frac{5}{6}$ hour

27. $6\frac{1}{3}$ hours

Answers for Spiral Review, page 352

1. Red: 0.6, $\frac{3}{5}$, 60%

Green: 0.25, $\frac{1}{4}$, 25%

Blue: 0.1, $\frac{1}{10}$, 10%

Purple: 0.05, $\frac{1}{20}$, 5%

2. $121.90

3. 4

4. 2

5. 18

6. 7

7. 15

8. $\frac{41}{3}$ or $13\frac{2}{3}$

9. $\frac{30}{7}$ or $4\frac{2}{7}$

10. $\frac{126}{5}$ or $25\frac{1}{5}$

Passport to Mathematics Book 1

Answers for Communicating About Mathematics, page 353

1. Answers vary.

   Longest to shortest: red-banded tree frog $= 2\frac{14}{20}$ in.,

   foam-nest tree frog $= 2\frac{7}{20}$ in.,

   ornate tree frog $= 1\frac{8}{10}$ in.,

   stripeless tree frog $= 1\frac{5}{10}$ in.

2. Longer; answers vary.

3. $2\frac{7}{10} - 1\frac{1}{2} = 2\frac{7}{10} - 1\frac{5}{10} = 1\frac{2}{10} = 1\frac{1}{5}$ in.

4. No, because the line would be $8\frac{7}{20}$ inches which is less than $11\frac{4}{5}$ inches.

5. $1\frac{1}{2} + \frac{3}{10} = 1\frac{5}{10} + \frac{3}{10} = 1\frac{8}{10} = 1\frac{4}{5}$ in.

Answers for Lesson 7.7, pages 355–357

Practice and Problem Solving

1. C

3. A

2. D

4. B

5. Remaining teams

6. $\frac{1}{20}$; subtract $\frac{3}{10}$ from $\frac{14}{40}$.

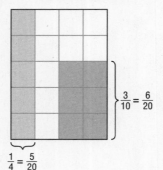

$\frac{3}{10} = \frac{6}{20}$

$\frac{1}{4} = \frac{5}{20}$

7. 1, it represents the whole amount of tickets.

8. $58\frac{3}{8}$ dollars per share

11. 59 in.; 64 in.

9. $54\frac{1}{8}$ dollars per share

12. 4 ft 11 in.; 5 ft 4 in.

13. 5 in.

10. a. $14\frac{3}{4}$ ft

b. $14\frac{11}{12}$ ft

c. 40 years ago

14. Quarter horse; quarter horse can run $\frac{1}{4}$ mile in about 20 seconds; thoroughbred can run $\frac{1}{4}$ mile in about 22 seconds.

15. B

16. $\frac{11}{27}$; $\frac{3}{55}$

Answers for Chapter Review, pages 359–361

1. $1\frac{1}{8}$ in.

2. 1 ft 3 in.

3. 2 ft 3 in.

4. 1 ft 7 in.

5. 2 ft 10 in.

6. $\frac{8}{20}$, $\frac{5}{20}$

7. $\frac{20}{28}$, $\frac{21}{28}$

8. $\frac{2}{16}$, $\frac{3}{16}$

9. $\frac{11}{12}$, $\frac{4}{12}$

10. $1\frac{1}{2}$ miles

11. $6\frac{6}{7}$

12. $4\frac{13}{24}$

13. $3\frac{4}{9}$

14. $4\frac{1}{3}$

15. $8\frac{2}{9}$

16. $\frac{1}{2}$ in.

17. $\frac{1}{3}$ h

18. $1\frac{3}{10}$

19. $2\frac{3}{4}$ in.

20. Toilet

21. $\frac{1}{4}$; it is $\frac{3}{40}$ more.

22. The sum is 1. All uses of water are listed in the table.

Answers for Chapter Test, page 362

1. 4
2. 144
3. 18
4. 6
5. 24
6. 20
7. $3\frac{1}{2}$ ft
8. $2\frac{1}{8}$ m
9. $3\frac{1}{2}$ mi
10. $1\frac{1}{5}$
11. $\frac{7}{9}$
12. $\frac{4}{12}$ or $\frac{1}{3}$
13. $\frac{13}{16}$
14. $\frac{29}{30}$
15. $\frac{7}{24}$
16. Neither; $1\frac{1}{4}$
17. Regroup; $4\frac{2}{3}$
18. Rename; $1\frac{3}{10}$
19. Both; $1\frac{5}{12}$
20. Regroup; $1\frac{7}{9}$
21. Rename; $3\frac{4}{15}$
22. 26.1 million
23. 10.5 million
24. 2.6 million
25. 79.6 million

Answers for Standardized Test Practice, page 363

1. D
2. D
3. D
4. C
5. D
6. C
7. A

Answers for Lesson 8.1, pages 371–373

Ongoing Assessment

1. $\frac{3}{4} \times 8 = \frac{3 \times 8}{4}$
   $= \frac{24}{4}$
   $= 6$

2. $\frac{4}{7} \times 3 = \frac{4 \times 3}{7}$
   $= \frac{12}{7}$
   $= 1\frac{5}{7}$

3. $\frac{5}{8} \times 4 = \frac{5 \times 4}{8}$
   $= \frac{20}{8}$
   $= \frac{5}{2}$
   $= 2\frac{1}{2}$

Practice and Problem Solving

1. $\frac{5}{6} \times 2 = 1\frac{2}{3}$

2. $3\frac{3}{4}$

3. Yes; commutative property of multiplication

4. Both the numerator and denominator were multiplied by 6, instead of only numerator.
   $\frac{2}{3} \times 6 = \frac{12}{3} = 4$

5. 8

6. $\frac{4}{6} \times 3 = \frac{12}{6} = 2$

7. $\frac{2}{3} \times 4 = \frac{8}{3} = 2\frac{2}{3}$

8. $\frac{6}{7}$

9. $\frac{2}{3}$

10. $1\frac{1}{4}$

11. $1\frac{1}{3}$

12. $3\frac{3}{4}$

13. $2\frac{2}{11}$

14. 5

15. 6

16. 1

(continued)

Answers for Lesson 8.1, pages 371–373 (cont.)

17. 4

18. 8

19. *G*

20. *K*

21. *E*

22. *H*

23. *J*

24. *A*

25. *Sample answer:* $\frac{5}{6} \times 5$; $4\frac{1}{6}$

26. *Sample answer:* $\frac{2}{7} \times 3$; $\frac{6}{7}$

27. *Sample answer:* $\frac{1}{9} \times 9$

28. Day shift only: 16
Evening shift only: 10
Night shift only: 9
Rotating shifts: 15

29. Coho salmon: 24 in.
Rainbow trout: 14 in.

30. D

31. Answers vary.

Passport to Mathematics Book 1

Answers for Lesson 8.2, pages 377–379

Ongoing Assessment

1. $\frac{4}{5} \times \frac{2}{3} = \frac{4 \times 2}{5 \times 3}$
$\qquad = \frac{8}{15}$

2. $\frac{3}{4} \times \frac{1}{6} = \frac{3 \times 1}{4 \times 6}$
$\qquad = \frac{3}{24}$
$\qquad = \frac{1}{8}$

3. $\frac{5}{6} \times \frac{6}{5} = \frac{5 \times 6}{6 \times 5}$
$\qquad = \frac{30}{30}$
$\qquad = 1$

Practice and Problem Solving

1. $\frac{3}{8}$ cup

2. $\frac{5}{21}$

3. $\frac{9}{20}$

4. **a.** 7   **b.** 3

5. You forgot to multiply the denominator; $\frac{8}{9} \times \frac{2}{9} = \frac{16}{81}$.

6. D; $\frac{5}{12}$

7. C; $\frac{5}{12}$

8. A; $\frac{3}{8}$

9. B; $\frac{21}{50}$

10. $\frac{8}{25}$

11. $\frac{7}{48}$

12. $\frac{15}{28}$

13. $\frac{8}{27}$

14. $\frac{9}{25}$

15. $\frac{3}{20}$

16. $\frac{2}{27}$

17. $\frac{1}{4}$

18. 3

19. 4

20. 7

21. 7

(continued)

Answers for Lesson 8.2, pages 377–379 (cont.)

22. $\frac{1}{2}$

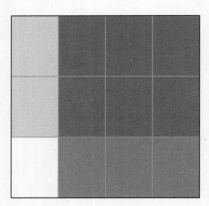

23. $\frac{8}{15}$

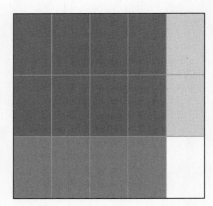

24. True; $\frac{1}{3} + \frac{1}{3} = \frac{2}{3}$, and $\frac{1}{3} \times \frac{1}{3} = \frac{1}{9}$, so $\frac{2}{3} > \frac{1}{9}$.

25. *Sample answers:* $\frac{2}{5} \times \frac{4}{9}, \frac{4}{5} \times \frac{2}{9}, \frac{1}{3} \times \frac{8}{15}, \frac{2}{3} \times \frac{4}{15}$

26. $\frac{1}{24}$ ft

27. $\frac{1}{12}$ ft

28. $\frac{1}{4}$ ft

29. Multiply measurement in feet by 12 to get inches.

Egg Type	ft	in.
Ostrich	$\frac{1}{2}$	6
Chickadee	$\frac{1}{24}$	$\frac{1}{2}$
Blue jay	$\frac{1}{12}$	1
Bald eagle	$\frac{1}{4}$	3

30. C

31. $\frac{7}{10} \times \frac{7}{10} = \frac{49}{100}$; $0.7 \times 0.7 = 0.49$; $0.49 = \frac{49}{100}$
They are the same.

32. Answers vary.

Passport to Mathematics Book 1

Answers for Spiral Review, page 380

1. $39\frac{1}{2}$ mi/h

2. a. $1\frac{1}{4}, \frac{5}{4}$ d. $3\frac{1}{8}, \frac{25}{8}$

   b. $1\frac{3}{4}, \frac{7}{4}$ e. $3\frac{1}{2}, \frac{7}{2}$

   c. $2\frac{3}{8}, \frac{19}{8}$

3. 16.65

4. 53.63

5. 60

6. 50

7. 1

8. 5

9. 28

10. 48

11. $\frac{5}{3}$ or $1\frac{2}{3}$

12. $\frac{5}{6}$

13. $\frac{1}{4}$

14. $\frac{1}{8}$

Answers for Lesson 8.3, pages 385–387

Ongoing Assessment

1. Chun's distance is $3\frac{3}{8}$ miles, so he ran the farthest.

2. Charles' distance is $2\frac{1}{2}$ miles, so he tied with Josh and Dionne.

Practice and Problem Solving

1. $2\frac{1}{2} \times 3\frac{1}{3} = 8\frac{1}{3}$

2. $2\frac{1}{7} \times 2\frac{1}{3} = \frac{15}{7} \times \frac{7}{3}$ Improper fractions

           $= \frac{105}{21}$ Multiply.

           $= 5$ Simplify.

3. Did not change to improper fractions first;
$2\frac{2}{3} \times 3\frac{4}{5} = \frac{8}{3} \times \frac{19}{5} = \frac{152}{15} = 10\frac{2}{15}$

4. Did not change to improper fractions first;
$4 \times 3\frac{3}{4} = 4 \times \frac{15}{4} = \frac{60}{4} = 15$

5. $2\frac{2}{3}$ h or 2 h 40 min

6. $1\frac{3}{4}$ h or 1 h 45 min

7. $\frac{5}{2} \times \frac{5}{2} = \frac{25}{4}$ or $6\frac{1}{4}$

8. $\frac{5}{2} \times \frac{5}{3} = \frac{25}{6}$ or $4\frac{1}{6}$

9. $6\frac{3}{4}$

10. $4\frac{1}{3}$

11. $\frac{6}{7}$

12. $2\frac{13}{16}$

13. 16

14. $3\frac{4}{15}$

15. $8\frac{1}{4}$

16. $9\frac{11}{21}$

17. $2\frac{11}{27}$ yd^2

18. $22\frac{2}{3}$ ft^2

19. $1\frac{1}{2}$ mi^2

20. Yes; $2\frac{1}{4} \times 3\frac{4}{5} = \frac{171}{20}$ or $8\frac{11}{20}$

(continued)

Answers for Lesson 8.3, pages 385–387 (cont.)

21. $\frac{21}{2}$ or $10\frac{1}{2}$, $\frac{28}{2}$ or 14, $\frac{35}{2}$ or $17\frac{1}{2}$;

each answer increases by $3\frac{1}{2}$.

$3\frac{1}{2} \times 6 = 21; 3\frac{1}{2} \times 7 = 24\frac{1}{2}$

22. $\frac{8}{21}$, $\frac{9}{21}$, $\frac{10}{21}$; each answer increases by $\frac{1}{21}$.

$1\frac{4}{7} \times \frac{1}{3} = \frac{11}{21}; 1\frac{5}{7} \times \frac{1}{3} = \frac{12}{21}$

23. $1\frac{1}{2}$, $2\frac{3}{4}$, 4; each answer increases by $1\frac{1}{4}$.

$4\frac{1}{5} \times 1\frac{1}{4} = 5\frac{1}{4}; 5\frac{1}{5} \times 1\frac{1}{4} = 6\frac{1}{2}$

24. Course 5

25. $112\frac{14}{15}$ mi

26. D

27. a. $69\frac{3}{8}$ in.^{2}

b. Answers vary.

Answers for Lesson 8.4, pages 391–394

Ongoing Assessment	
1. 10	**2.** 6

Practice and Problem Solving

1. $2\frac{2}{3} \div \frac{2}{3}$

2. $1\frac{1}{6} \div \frac{5}{6}$

3. $\frac{3}{5}$

4. $\frac{15}{9}$ or $1\frac{2}{3}$

5. Answers vary.

6. $1\frac{4}{5} \div \frac{3}{5}$

7. $1\frac{3}{4} \div \frac{1}{2}$

8. 4

9. $\frac{1}{7}$

10. $2\frac{3}{7}$

11. $6\frac{1}{3}$

12. $5\frac{3}{4}$

13. 32

14. $9\frac{2}{3}$

15. $4\frac{7}{8}$

16. Greater than 1

17. Less than 1

18. Greater than 1

19. Greater than 1

20. Greater than 1

21. Less than 1

22. $\frac{11}{6}$ or $1\frac{5}{6}$

23. $\frac{13}{4}$ or $3\frac{1}{4}$

24. $\frac{3}{4}$

25. 3

26. 5 and $\frac{2}{5}$ of another.

27. $w = 112\frac{1}{2}$, $x = 56\frac{1}{4}$, $y = 45$, and $z = 15$; work backward.

28. A

29. C

30. A

31. 19 bags; answers vary.

32. Answers vary.

33. Answers vary.

34. $1\frac{5}{8}$

Answers for Spiral Review, page 394

1. $=$

2. $<$

3. $>$

4. $\begin{array}{r} 63.8 \\ +\ 20.4 \\ \hline 84.2 \end{array}$

5. $\begin{array}{r} 15.29 \\ -\ \ 4.37 \\ \hline 10.92 \end{array}$

6. Answers vary; bar graph or pictograph

7. $\frac{8}{16}$

8. $\frac{6}{15}$

9. $\frac{4}{28}$

10. $\frac{1}{3}$ mi

Answers for Mid-Chapter Assessment, page 395

1. $\frac{3}{4}$

2. $2\frac{6}{7}$

3. $\frac{5}{18}$

4. $\frac{1}{8}$

5. $4\frac{4}{21}$

6. $1\frac{1}{5}$

7. 18

8. $8\frac{2}{3}$

9. 3

10. 12

11. 2

12. 9

13. $\frac{6}{7}$

14. 1

15. $1\frac{4}{5}$ yd^2

16. $\frac{7}{20}$ mi^2

17. 30 ft^2

18. 2

19. $\frac{1}{6}$

20. $1\frac{1}{3}$

21. 3

22. 9

23. $2\frac{2}{3}$

24. $\frac{1}{3}$

25. $6\frac{2}{3}$

26. Banana: 8; chocolate: 18; vanilla: 16; butterscotch: 6

27. 6

Answers for Lesson 8.5, pages 397–399

Ongoing Assessment

1. $2\frac{1}{2}$ **2.** 2

Practice and Problem Solving

1. $\frac{5}{7}$

2. 9

3. To divide, you *multiply* by the reciprocal of the divisor.

$$\frac{7}{8} \div \frac{5}{6} = \frac{7}{8} \times \frac{6}{5}$$
$$= \frac{42}{40} = 1\frac{1}{20}$$

4. To divide, you multiply by the *reciprocal* of the divisor.

$$\frac{5}{9} \div \frac{3}{5} = \frac{5}{9} \times \frac{5}{3} = \frac{25}{27}$$

5. 1 mi longer

6. $1\frac{2}{3}$ times longer

7. $\frac{5}{4}$

8. $\frac{9}{7}$

9. $\frac{6}{11}$

10. 8

11. $3\frac{3}{4}$

12. $2\frac{1}{4}$

13. $1\frac{3}{4}$

14. $1\frac{1}{3}$

15. $4\frac{1}{5}$

16. $1\frac{11}{15}$

17. $13\frac{1}{5}$

18. $4\frac{1}{2}$

19. 126 pieces

20. $18\frac{1}{2}$ servings

21. $\frac{14}{8}, \frac{21}{8}, \frac{28}{8}$; the numerator of the improper fraction increases by 7.

22. $\frac{36}{8}, \frac{45}{10}, \frac{54}{12}$; the numerators of the improper fractions increase by 9, the denominators of the improper fraction increase by 2, and the value of x is $4\frac{1}{2}$.

(continued)

Answers for Lesson 8.5, pages 397–399 (cont.)

23. $\frac{1}{4}, \frac{1}{3}, \frac{1}{2}$; the denominators of the simplified fractions decrease by 1.

24. 11

25. B

26. B

27. a. 16 bags per hour

   b. Answers vary.

Answers for Lesson 8.6, pages 401–404

Ongoing Assessment

1. $3\frac{3}{4} \div 5 = \frac{15}{4} \div 5$

$\phantom{3\frac{3}{4} \div 5} = \frac{15}{4} \times \frac{1}{5}$

$\phantom{3\frac{3}{4} \div 5} = \frac{15}{20}$

$\phantom{3\frac{3}{4} \div 5} = \frac{3}{4}$

2. $6 \div 1\frac{1}{3} = 6 \div \frac{4}{3}$

$\phantom{6 \div 1\frac{1}{3}} = 6 \times \frac{3}{4}$

$\phantom{6 \div 1\frac{1}{3}} = \frac{18}{4}$

$\phantom{6 \div 1\frac{1}{3}} = 4\frac{2}{4}$

$\phantom{6 \div 1\frac{1}{3}} = 4\frac{1}{2}$

3. $3\frac{1}{2} \div 1\frac{1}{4} = \frac{7}{2} \div \frac{5}{4}$

$\phantom{3\frac{1}{2} \div 1\frac{1}{4}} = \frac{7}{2} \times \frac{4}{5}$

$\phantom{3\frac{1}{2} \div 1\frac{1}{4}} = \frac{28}{10}$

$\phantom{3\frac{1}{2} \div 1\frac{1}{4}} = 2\frac{8}{10}$

$\phantom{3\frac{1}{2} \div 1\frac{1}{4}} = 2\frac{4}{5}$

Practice and Problem Solving

1. $2\frac{3}{5} \div 6 = \frac{13}{5} \div \frac{6}{1}$ Rewrite as improper fractions.

$\phantom{2\frac{3}{5} \div 6} = \frac{13}{5} \times \frac{1}{6}$ Multiply by reciprocal.

$\phantom{2\frac{3}{5} \div 6} = \frac{13}{30}$ Multiply fractions.

2. $4\frac{2}{3} \div 3\frac{1}{2} = \frac{14}{3} \div \frac{7}{2}$ Rewrite as improper fractions.

$\phantom{4\frac{2}{3} \div 3\frac{1}{2}} = \frac{14}{3} \times \frac{2}{7}$ Multiply by reciprocal.

$\phantom{4\frac{2}{3} \div 3\frac{1}{2}} = \frac{28}{21}$ Multiply fractions.

$\phantom{4\frac{2}{3} \div 3\frac{1}{2}} = \frac{4}{3}$ or $1\frac{1}{3}$ Simplify.

3. $5 \div 3\frac{3}{4} = \frac{20}{4} \div \frac{15}{4}$ or $5 \div 3\frac{3}{4} = \frac{5}{1} \div \frac{15}{4} = \frac{5}{1} \times \frac{4}{15}$

$\phantom{5 \div 3\frac{3}{4}} = \frac{20}{15} = \frac{4}{3}$, or $1\frac{1}{3}$ $= \frac{20}{15} = \frac{4}{3}$, or $1\frac{1}{3}$

(continued)

Answers for Lesson 8.6, pages 401–404 (cont.)

4. $\frac{1}{8}$; each student gets $\frac{1}{8}$ of a cake.

5. Yes; finding the reciprocal of the first fraction gives an incorrect answer.

$$\frac{14}{3} \div \frac{7}{2} = \frac{14}{3} \times \frac{2}{7} = \frac{4}{3} \text{ or } 1\frac{1}{3}$$

$$\frac{14}{3} \div \frac{7}{2} = \frac{3}{14} \times \frac{7}{2} = \frac{3}{4}$$

6. $4\frac{9}{10}$ oz

7. $\frac{9}{10}$ cup

8. $\frac{23}{24}$ cup

9. $2\frac{1}{4}$; $2\frac{1}{4} \div 3 = \frac{3}{4}$

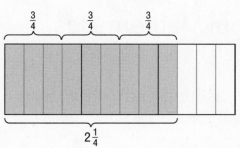

10. C

11. D

12. A

13. B

14. $\frac{21}{25}$

15. $5\frac{1}{3}$

16. $\frac{5}{6}$

17. $\frac{16}{19}$

18. $\frac{5}{6}$

19. $\frac{19}{20}$

20. $1\frac{13}{14}$

21. $1\frac{3}{4}$

22. $24\frac{2}{3}$

23. Sometimes

24. Sometimes

25. Sometimes

26. $10\frac{1}{2}$ minutes

27. 21 minutes

28. 2 times more

29. $3\frac{1}{9}$

30. $5\frac{1}{9}$

31. $3\frac{11}{24}$ in.

32. C

33. B

34. No, it will take you $3\frac{7}{9}$ hours which is more than $3\frac{1}{2}$ hours.

35. 3 mi marker; you will have $\frac{5}{6}$ h extra time.

Answers for Spiral Review, page 404

1.

$$6 \xrightarrow{\times 3} 18 \xrightarrow{\div 6} 3 \xrightarrow{+9} 12 \xrightarrow{-4} 8$$

2.

$$10 \xrightarrow{-5} 5 \xrightarrow{\div 2} 2.5 \xrightarrow{\times 6} 15 \xrightarrow{\div 4} 3.75$$

3. 15.3

4. 18.55

5. 7.4

6. 17.08

7. 0.68

8. 75

9. 3

10. $4\frac{1}{5}$

11. 39

12. 21

13. 70

14. $3\frac{3}{4}$ lb

Answers for Communicating About Mathematics, page 405

1. The bee hummingbird's beak is about $\frac{1}{5}$ as long as its full length.

$$2\frac{1}{4} \times \frac{1}{5} = \frac{9}{20}$$

The beak is $\frac{9}{20}$ in. long.

2. $3\frac{7}{9}$

3. $\frac{2}{25}$

4. Eats: $\frac{4}{5}$ grams

Drinks: $12\frac{4}{5}$ grams

5. Human heart beats $1\frac{1}{3}$ times per second.

6. 240 breaths per minute

Copyright © McDougal Littell Inc. All rights reserved.

162 *Answer Masters*

Passport to Mathematics Book 1

Answers for Lesson 8.7, pages 407–409

Ongoing Assessment

1. 5 lb   **2.** 150 lb

Practice and Problem Solving

1. C

2. A

3. B

4. Yes; a right angle is 90°.

5. No; none of the angles are 90°.

6. No; none of the angles are 90°.

7. Answers vary.

8. $3\frac{3}{4}$ cm^2

9. 7 cm^2

10. $6\frac{7}{8}$ cm^2

11. a. $\frac{1}{8}$ units^2 **b.** $\frac{1}{2}$ units^2

c. $1\frac{1}{8}$ units^2 **d.** 2 units^2

Pattern: $\frac{1}{8}, \frac{4}{8}, \frac{9}{8}, \frac{16}{8}$; numerators increase by consecutive odd numbers as both legs increase by 0.5.

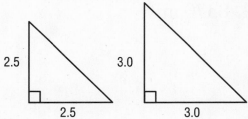

12. 8 in.

13. 4 cm

14. 0.6 m

15. 60 trees

16. C

17. 24 m^2

18. 30 in.^{2}

19. 20 cm^2

20. D

21. $1\frac{1}{2}$ units^2 and $2\frac{1}{2}$ units$^2 = 4$ units^2; sum the base first, then find the area of the large triangle.

22. Answers vary.

1. Pencils: 24; pens: 6;
   markers: 2

2. $2\frac{5}{8}$

3. $4\frac{1}{2}$

4. $\frac{1}{3}$

5. $\frac{1}{8}$

6. $\frac{8}{21}$

7. $\frac{7}{40}$

8. $\frac{19}{100}$

9. $\frac{3}{5}$

10. Red maple: $22\frac{1}{2}$ m

    Quaken aspen: $18\frac{3}{4}$ m

11. 7

12. $1\frac{1}{3}$

13. $\frac{11}{18}$

14. $9\frac{1}{2}$

15. 12

16. $\frac{15}{16}$

17. $5\frac{2}{5}$

18. $1\frac{3}{5}$

19. $5\frac{1}{3}$

20. $1\frac{7}{18}$

21. $2\frac{1}{6}$

22. $16\frac{2}{3}$

23. $\frac{2}{9}$ ft^2

24. 8370 mi^2

Answers for Chapter Assessment, page 414

1. $2\frac{1}{2}$

2. $5\frac{7}{10}$

3. 4

4. False; $3 \times \frac{1}{4} = \frac{3}{4}$

5. True

6. $\frac{1}{8}$

7. $2\frac{2}{5}$

8. $\frac{19}{27}$

9. $10\frac{5}{24}$

10. $2\frac{1}{5}$

11. $9\frac{1}{3}$

12. $4\frac{7}{12}$

13. $3\frac{15}{17}$

14. $8\frac{11}{18}$ m^2

15. $\frac{63}{128}$ cm^2

16. $1\frac{7}{48}$ mi^2

17. $\frac{8}{125}$

18. 2 times

19. $2\frac{1}{6}$ ft; $\frac{13}{16}$ ft

20. $2\frac{2}{3}$ times longer;
    $2\frac{2}{3}$ times longer;
    Yes, they both have the same
    length-to-width ratio.

Answers for Standardized Test Practice, page 415

1. D

2. A

3. B

4. B

5. B

6. C

7. D

8. A

9. D

Ongoing Assessment

1.–4. Answers vary.

Practice and Problem Solving

1. No; one side is curved.

2. Yes; pentagon

3. Yes; hexagon

4. a. Start at *A*, move up 2 to *B*, right 6 to *C*, down 2 to *D*, and left 6 to *A*.

b. Start at *R*, move left 3 and up 1 to *S*, right 5 and up 1 to *T*, right 2 and down 1 to *U*, and left 4 and down 1 to *R*.

5. About 12 units

6.–9. Answers vary.

10.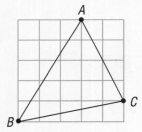

11.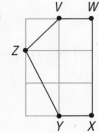

12. From *P*, move down 3 and right 2 to *R*, right 2, up 2 to *Q*, up 1, left 4 to *P*.

13. From *J*, move right 1, down 2 to *N*, right 3 to *M*, left 1, up 3 to *L*, left 2 to *K*, left 1, down 1 to *J*.

14. From *A*, move right 1 and down 2 to *D*, right 4 and up 3 to *C*, left 2 to *B*, left 3 and down 1 to *A*.

(continued)

Passport to Mathematics Book 1

Answers for Lesson 9.1, pages 421–423 (cont.)

15. *Sample answer:*

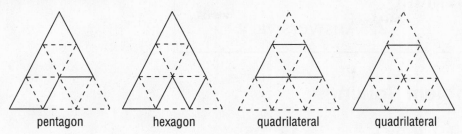

pentagon   hexagon   quadrilateral   quadrilateral

16. 13

17. 6 units^2

18. 8 units^2

19. 10 units^2

20. D

21. C

22. Back:

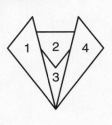

3 triangles: 1, 4, 2, and 3
1 quadrilateral: 3
3 pentagons: 2, 1 and 2 and 3, 2 and 3 and 4
2 hexagons: 1 and 3, 3 and 4
1 heptagon: 1 and 2 and 3 and 4
3 octagons: 1 and 2, 1 and 3 and 4, 2 and 4

Front:

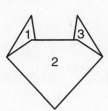

2 quadrilaterals: 1, 3
1 pentagon: 2
2 hexagons: 1 and 2, 2 and 3
1 heptagon: 1 and 2 and 3

Answers for Lesson 9.2, pages 427–429

Ongoing Assessment

1. Answers vary.   2. Answers vary.

Practice and Problem Solving

1. $\angle QPR$, $\angle P$, or $\angle RPQ$

2. $\overrightarrow{PQ}$ and $\overrightarrow{PR}$

3. P

4. Answers vary.

5. Answers vary.

6. About $48°$

7. B

8. A

9. C

10. $80°$

11. $125°$

12. $40°$

13. $60°$

14. $90°$

15. $175°$

16. $45°$

17. $15°$

18. $95°$

19. $360°$; it is a complete turn.

20. Obtuse

21. Fold the paper from top to bottom, then fold it again from left to right so the first fold lines match. The corner where the two folds meet is a right angle that can be used to measure.

22. a. Acute
    b. Right
    c. Obtuse

23. $135°$, $45°$; $180°$

24. a. Obtuse; so they add to $180°$.
    b. Right; so they add to $180°$.

25. C

26. A: acute; B: acute; C: right; D: acute; E: acute; F: obtuse; G: obtuse

Answers for Spiral Review, page 430

1. $\frac{3}{4}$

2. $\frac{1}{5}$

3. $\frac{37}{100}$

4. $\frac{59}{100}$

5. 54

6. 1000

7. 300

8. 100

9. 7600

10. 0.057

11. 32, 29

12. 69, 74

13. 7, 7

14. Yes

15. No

16. Yes

17. Blue jay: 30 cm;
American robin: 24 cm;
Northern cardinal: 20 cm;
House sparrow: 15 cm

Answers for Communicating About Mathematics, page 431

1. Yes

2. **a.** Quadrilateral
   b. Triangle
   c. Pentagon
   d. Quadrilateral

3. Answers vary.

4. *Sample answer:* $\angle FAJ = \angle GAK$; the triangles are acute.

5. $22°$, $24°$, $134°$; the sum of the angles in a triangle is $180°$.

Answers for Lesson 9.3, pages 433–435

Ongoing Assessment

1. Draw a triangle with the same side lengths.

2. Answers vary.

Practice and Problem Solving

1. C

2. D

3. B

4. A

5. Answers vary.

6. No; side measures are different. Yes; the figures are the same shape.

7. Answers vary.

8. A and D

9. A and C

10. $a = 2.8, b = 45°, c = 90°,$ $d = 2, e = 45°$

11. $a = 90°, b = 6.8, c = 90°,$ $d = 4$

12. Yes; no;

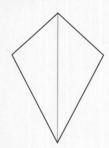

13. Yes; yes;

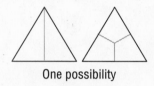

One possibility

14. No; no

15. Yes; yes;

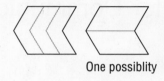

One possiblity

16. No; to change an angle, you need to change the length of 2 of the sides.

17. a: triangle; b: triangle; c: right triangle

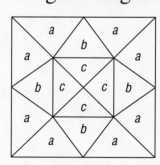

(continued)

Answers for Lesson 9.3, pages 433–435 (cont.)

18. Answers vary.

19. B

20. Steps 1 and 2; triangles AEB and AFC, triangles AEG and AFH, triangles AED and AFD, triangles AGD and AHD, triangles EBD and FCD

Answers for Lesson 9.4, pages 439–442

Ongoing Assessment

1. Answers vary.

2. If you trace a shape on paper, you can check for lines of symmetry by folding the paper in half through the center of the figure. If the two sides of the figure match up, then a line of symmetry exists there.

Practice and Problem Solving

1.–3. Answers vary.

4.

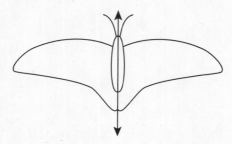

5. Answers vary.

6.

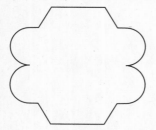

7. No

8. No

9. Yes;

10. Yes;

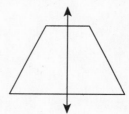

11. No; flipping about the line doesn't produce an identical figure.

(continued)

Answers for Lesson 9.4, pages 439–442 (cont.)

12. Yes; the flipped figure lands directly on itself.

13. No; flipping about the line changes the position of the circle.

14. Answers vary.

15. Yes; 2

16. Yes; 1

17. No

18.

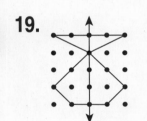

19.

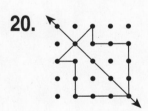

20.

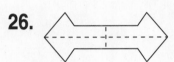

21. 3 lines

22. 4 lines

23. No lines

24.

25.

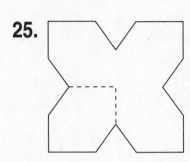

26.

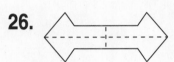

27. B

28. Yes; vertical line through the center of the face. No; ears do not have a line of symmetry.

Answers for Spiral Review, page 442

1. 5

2. 6.01, 6.05, 6.051, 6.15, 6.5

3. $\frac{1}{2}, \frac{4}{7}, \frac{5}{7}, \frac{5}{6}$

4. $7\frac{9}{10}$

5. $2\frac{1}{4}$

6. $\frac{14}{15}$

7. 3

8. Triangle; $\angle A$ acute, $\angle B$ right, $\angle C$ acute

9. Quadrilateral; $\angle M$ obtuse, $\angle N$ right, $\angle K$ right, $\angle L$ acute

10. Kite; $\angle T$ obtuse, $\angle U$ right, $\angle R$ obtuse, $\angle S$ acute

Answers for Mid-Chapter Assessment, page 443

1. From *A*, move right 4, up 1 to *B*, left 2, up 3 to *C*, left 2, down 4 to *A*.

2. From *A*, move right 4, up 3 to *B*, left 3, up 3 to *C*, left 2, down 1 to *D*, right 1, down 5 to *A*.

3. From *A*, move right 1, down 1 to *B*, right 2 to *C*, right 2, up 2 to *D*, left 5, up 2 to *E*, down 3 to *A*.

4. **a.** quadrilateral
   b. triangle
   c. right triangle
   d. pentagon
   e. quadrilateral

5. Right; 90°

6. Acute; 60°

7. Obtuse; 120°

8. Neither; different size and shape.

9. Similar; side lengths are different but same shape.

10. Congruent and similar; angle measures and side lengths are the same.

11. 1 line

12. 1 line

13. 2 lines

14.

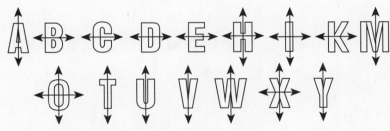

Answers for Lesson 9.5, pages 447–449

Ongoing Assessment

1.–3.

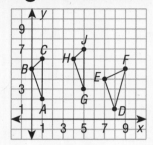

4. Yes; you can slide triangle ABC 4 units to the right and 1 unit up to become triangle GHJ.

Practice and Problem Solving

1. coordinate plane

2. y-axis

3. $(4, 3)$

4. x-coordinate; it shows the position along the x-axis.

5. Answers vary.

6.

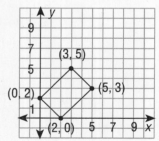

   Rectangle, quadrilateral

7. R

8. T

9. S

10. P

11.

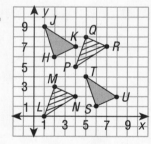

Shaded figures are slides.
Striped figures are slides.

12.

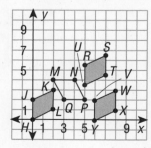

Shaded figures are slides.

(continued)

Answers for Lesson 9.5, pages 447–449 (cont.)

13. Yes; it has the same side lengths and the same angle measures.

14. No; the side lengths are different.

15. Left 2, down 5

16. Right 3, up 3

17. Left 2, up 1

18. (3, 2), (3, 0), (5, 2)

19.

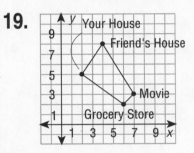

20. A

21. 180° rotation

22. Slide

23. About a 90° rotation

24. Slide

25. Answers vary.

Answers for Lesson 9.6, pages 451–454

Ongoing Assessment

1. No, a triangle cannot be formed with more than one right angle. No, a triangle cannot be formed with more than one obtuse angle.

2. In a right triangle, the other two angles are acute. In an obtuse triangle, the other two angles are acute.

Practice and Problem Solving

1. Right, isosceles

2. Obtuse, scalene

3. Acute, isosceles, equilateral

4.–6. Answers vary.

7. Isosceles; 4 cm, 4 cm, 2 cm

8. Scalene; 1.5 cm, 3.5 cm, 4 cm

9. Equilateral; all sides are 2.5 cm.

10.–13. Answers vary.

14. Isosceles, acute

15. Scalene, right

16. Scalene, acute

17. Answers vary.

18. 60°, 90°, 30°; Right

19. 125°, 20°, 35°; Obtuse

20. 70°, 80°, 30°; Acute

21. No

22. Yes

23. Yes

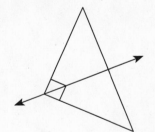

24. Yes

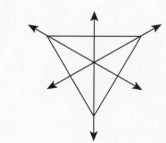

(continued)

178 *Answer Masters*

25. Never

26. Always

27. 2 right triangles, or 1 acute and 1 obtuse;

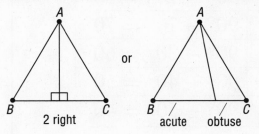

28. Equilateral

29. B

30. C

31. Answers vary.

32. Answers vary.

Answers for Spiral Review, page 454

1. $9 + 6 - 3 \times 5 = 0$

2. $7 + 8 \div 4 - 2 = 7$

3. $1 + 5 \times 9 \div 3 = 16$

4. 7.29 ft^2

5. 23.24 in.^2

6. 86.64 cm^2

7.

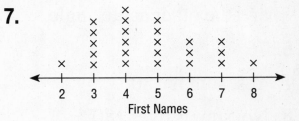

8. $4\frac{1}{2}$ lb

Answers for Lesson 9.7, pages 459–461

Ongoing Assessment

1.

Triangle	Measure $\angle A$	Measure $\angle C$	Measure $\angle B$
1	10°	90°	90° − 10° = 80°
2	20°	90°	90° − 20° = 70°
3	30°	90°	90° − 30° = 60°
4	40°	90°	90° − 40° = 50°
5	50°	90°	90° − 50° = 40°

2. Yes, answers vary.

Practice and Problem Solving

1. C

2. A

3. B

4. D

5. The measure of the third angle is 180° minus the sum of 90° and the other acute angle.

6. 76°

7. Yes, sum is 180°.

8. No, sum is over 180°.

9. Yes, sum is 180°.

10. 70° + 70° + 40° = 180°

11. 80° + 60° + 40° = 180°

12. 30° + 60° + 90° = 180°

13. 60°

14. 20°

15. 30°

16. a. 135°   **b.** 90°; 90°

17. 10°, 20°, 30°, 40°, 50°, 60°; as the measures of $\angle A$ and $\angle B$ decrease by 5° each, the measure of $\angle C$ increases by 10°.

18. A

19. D

20. The angles of the quadrilateral are the angles of 2 triangles, so they total 2 · 180° or 360°.

21. Answers vary. 360°

Answers for Chapter Review, pages 463–465

1. Each quadrilateral must have 4 sides.

2. No; not all of its sides are straight.

3. Yes; hexagon

4. Yes; pentagon

5. No; the figure is not closed.

6. $\angle W$, $\angle Z$

7. $\angle X$ **8.** $\angle Y$

9. Answers vary.

10. Answers vary.

11. Yes;

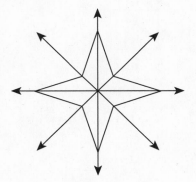

12. No line symmetry

13. Yes;

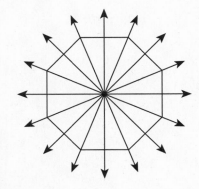

14. Yes;

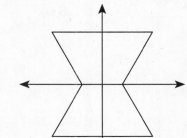

15.–18.

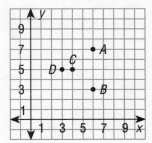

19. Equilateral

20. Scalene

21. Isosceles

22. Isosceles

23. Right

24. Acute

25. Obtuse

26. Acute

27. 30°

28. 60°

29. 89°

30. 33°

Answers for Chapter Assessment, page 466

1. D

2. C

3. A

4. B

5. 130°; obtuse

6. 90°; right

7. 70°; acute

8. $a = 5; b = 95°; c = 5; d = 95°; e = 4; f = 95°$

9. $a = 20°; b = 12; c = 35; d = 70°; e = 33$

10.

11.

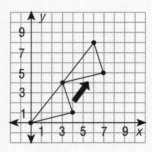

$(3, 4), (7, 5), (6, 8)$

12.

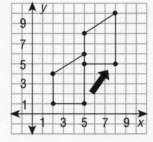

$(5, 5), (8, 5), (5, 8), (8, 10)$

13. Triangle ABC is equilateral, triangle BCD is isosceles; $x = 48°$

14. Triangles ABC, BCE, CDE, and ACD are scalene. Triangles ABE, ABD, EBD, and EAD are isosceles; $x = 53°$

Answers for Standardized Test Practice, page 467

1. B	**5.** D
2. B	**6.** C
3. D	**7.** D
4. C	**8.** A

Answers for Cumulative Review, pages 468 and 469

1. A. $1\frac{1}{8}$ in., $\frac{9}{8}$ in.

   B. $1\frac{3}{4}$ in., $\frac{7}{4}$ in.

   C. $2\frac{1}{4}$ in., $\frac{9}{4}$ in.

   D. $2\frac{5}{8}$ in., $\frac{21}{8}$ in.

   E. $3\frac{1}{2}$ in., $\frac{7}{2}$ in.

   F. $4\frac{7}{8}$ in., $\frac{39}{8}$ in.

2. $1\frac{1}{12}$

3. $6\frac{1}{2}$

4. $3\frac{3}{5}$

5. $2\frac{1}{6}$

6. $\frac{1}{5}$

7. $3\frac{1}{2}$

8. $4\frac{2}{5}$

9. $4\frac{2}{3}$

10. $5\frac{1}{6}$ cm

11. $3\frac{1}{4}$ m

12. $2\frac{4}{7}$ in.^{2}

13. $1\frac{1}{2}$ ft

14. 12 cm^2

15. $\frac{9}{14}$ mi^2

16. $\frac{1}{15}$

17. 12

18. $9 \times \frac{1}{10} = \frac{9}{10}$

19. $1\frac{1}{2} \div 6 = \frac{1}{4}$

20. $\frac{4}{5} \div \frac{3}{10} = 2\frac{2}{3}$

21. $2\frac{1}{6} \times \frac{6}{7} = 1\frac{6}{7}$

22. Right triangle; $\angle A$ is $50°$ acute, $\angle B$ is $40°$ acute, $\angle C$ is $90°$ right.

23. Pentagon; $\angle A$ is $55°$ acute, $\angle B$ is $135°$ obtuse, $\angle C$ is $120°$ obtuse, $\angle D$ is $90°$ right, $\angle E$ is $140°$ obtuse.

24. Quadrilateral; $\angle A$ is $85°$ acute, $\angle B$ is $55°$ acute, $\angle C$ is $145°$ obtuse, $\angle D$ is $75°$ acute.

(continued)

Answers for Cumulative Review, pages 468 and 469 (cont.)

25. A and B

26. A and D

27.–29. *Sample answers:*

27. 1;

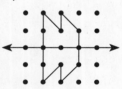

28. 2;

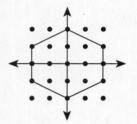

29. 1;

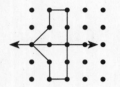

30.

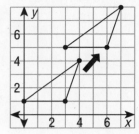

31.

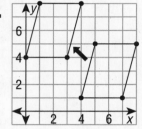

32.

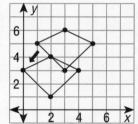

33. Acute angle; $30\frac{7}{12}$ yd

Answers for Lesson 10.1, pages 477–479

Ongoing Assessment

1. Line 1 and line 2, line 3 and line 4

2. Measure the distance between the lines in two different places. If the distance is equal, the lines are parallel.

Practice and Problem Solving

1. B **2.** C

3. A, B

4. True; this is the definition of perpendicular lines.

5. False; lines may cross at any angle.

6. Answers vary.

7. Parallel; they seem to stay the same distance apart.

8. Intersecting; you can see that they cross.

9. Parallel; they seem to stay the same distance apart.

10. Intersecting; you can see that if they were drawn longer, they would cross.

11. $\overleftrightarrow{EF}$ and $\overleftrightarrow{GH}$

12. *Sample answers:* $\overleftrightarrow{AB}$ and $\overleftrightarrow{CD}$, $\overleftrightarrow{EF}$ and $\overleftrightarrow{CD}$, $\overleftrightarrow{GH}$ and $\overleftrightarrow{CD}$, $\overleftrightarrow{EF}$ and $\overleftrightarrow{AB}$, $\overleftrightarrow{GH}$ and $\overleftrightarrow{AB}$

13. $\overleftrightarrow{CD}$

14. $\overleftrightarrow{AB}$ or $\overleftrightarrow{CD}$

15. Never

16. Sometimes

17. Always

18. $\overleftrightarrow{GH}$, $\overleftrightarrow{EF}$

19. $\overleftrightarrow{CD}$

20. $\overleftrightarrow{GH}$

21. Answers vary.

22. Base line and service line

23. Doubles sideline, singles and service sideline, center line

24. They meet at a right angle.

25. A

26. D

27. Answers vary.

Answers for Lesson 10.2, pages 481–483

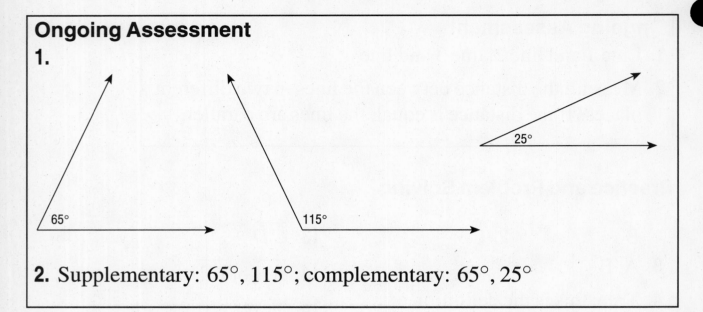

Ongoing Assessment

1.

65°   115°   25°

2. Supplementary: 65°, 115°; complementary: 65°, 25°

Practice and Problem Solving

1. Perpendicular

2. Complementary

3. 55°

4. 35°

5. *Sample answer:*
   ∠DFA and ∠AFC;
   ∠EFD and ∠CFE;
   ∠AFC and ∠CFB;
   ∠BFC and ∠DFB;
   ∠DFB and ∠AFD

6. Answers vary.

7. **a.** ∠1 and ∠3 are supplementary, so ∠3 is 55°.

   b. ∠3 and ∠4 are supplementary, so ∠4 is 125°.

   c. ∠1 and ∠4 both measure 125°, so they are congruent.

(continued)

8. $144°$

9. $25°$

10. $53°$

11. $88°$

12. $70°$;

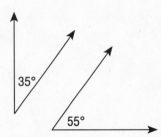

13. $35°$;

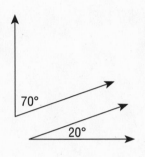

14. $60°$;

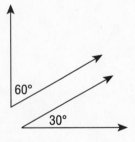

15. $20°$;

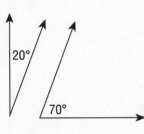

16. $20°$;

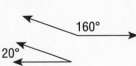

17. $80°$;

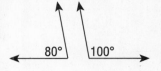

18. $140°$;

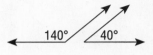

19. $150°$;

20. True; *Sample answer:* two angles whose measures sum to $90°$.

21. False; two right angles are supplementary.

22. $60°$; $\angle 3 = 90° - 30° = 60°$

23. $\angle 1$ and $\angle 2$ are congruent.

24. $\angle 2$ and $\angle 3$ are complementary angles.

25. $\angle 1$ and $\angle 3$ are complementary angles.

26. *Sample answer:* 9th St., Massachusetts Ave., and K St.

27. D

28. B

29. Answers vary.

Answers for Spiral Review, page 484

1. $\frac{3}{10}$

2. $\frac{16}{40} = \frac{2}{5}$

3. $\frac{2}{5}$

4. 0.8, 80%

5. 0.38, 38%

6. 0.67, 67%

7. 0.55, 55%

8. 0.79, 79%

9. a. 6 h

   b. $71.25

Answers for Lesson 10.3, pages 487–489

Ongoing Assessment

1. Answers vary.

2. 60°, 120°, 120°

3. If one angle of a parallelogram is 60°, then the opposite angle must be 60°. Since the sum of the four angles of a parallelogram is 360°, the sum of the other two angles is 360° − 120° = 240°. Since these other two angles are opposite, they must have the same measure, so 240° ÷ 2 = 120°.

Practice and Problem Solving

1. A, B, C, D

2. C

3. C, D

4. A, C, D

5. *Sample answers:*
   a. QRVU
   b. PQUT, PRVT, QRVU, QSVT
   c. PQUT, PRVT, QRVU
   d. PQUT, PRVT, QRVU, QSVT, QRVT, QSVU, PSVT

6. No; no; the four sides have the same length no matter how you move them, so they form a parallelogram, or if the angles are 90°, a square.

7. parallelogram, quadrilateral

8. quadrilateral

9. rectangle, parallelogram, quadrilateral

10. quadrilateral

11. True

12. False

13. False

14. True

(continued)

15. Yes

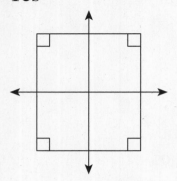

16. No

17. Yes

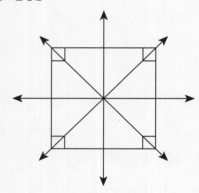

18. No

19. Rectangle; $x = 3$, $y = 8$, $z = 90°$

20. Both; $x = 2$, $y = 2$

21. Neither; $x = 4$, $y = 4$, $z = 65°$

22. No, opposite angles are not congruent; the streets do not form a parallelogram.

23. B

24. C

25. Answers vary.

Answers for Lesson 10.4, pages 493–496

Ongoing Assessment

1.–3. Answers vary.

Practice and Problem Solving

1. 24 units^2

2. 12 units^2

3. 9 units^2

4. Your friend used the length of a side instead of the height.

5. Triangles may vary, but the base × height should be 36.

6. 4 in.^{2}

7. 18 m^2

8. 15 cm^2

9. 26 in.^{2}

10. 40 ft^2

11. 5 cm, 3 cm; $7\frac{1}{2}$ cm^2

12. 4 cm, 3 cm; 6 cm^2

13. 72 units^2

14. 65 units^2

15. 48 units^2

16. 84 ft^2

17. 2 mi

18. 10 cm

19. a. 3 ft^2, 7.5 ft^2
   b. 546 ft^2

20. 110,400 mi^2

21. B

22. 2450 ft^2

23. Answers vary.

24. a. Answers vary.
   b. 6 people
   c. 6 units^2; they should be the same.

Answers for Spiral Review, page 496

1. 28

2. 60

3. 24

4. 35

5. 36

6. 14

7. 22

8. 60

9. 4

10. **a.**

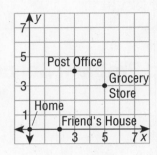

b. 2 blocks

Answers for Mid-Chapter Assessment, page 497

1. $\overleftrightarrow{GH}$

2. $\overleftrightarrow{AB}$

3. $\angle 2$

4. $\angle 4$

5. $\overleftrightarrow{EF}$ or $\overleftrightarrow{AB}$

6. $\angle 1$

7. Quadrilateral, parallelogram, rectangle

8. Quadrilateral, parallelogram

9. Quadrilateral, parallelogram, rectangle, square

10. Quadrilateral

11. 9 units^2

12. 21 units^2

13. Find the sum of the areas of the individual triangles. Or, use the formula $A = \frac{1}{2} \times$ base $\times$ height where the base is 10 and the height is 6.

14. False; quadrilaterals have four sides which are not necessarily parallel.

15. True; squares have four angles which measure $90°$.

16. True; all rectangles have four sides.

17. False; not all parallelograms have four angles which measure $90°$.

18. 12

19. 87 in.^{2}

20. 1044 in.^{2}

Answers for Lesson 10.5, pages 501–503

Ongoing Assessment

1. $C = \pi \cdot d = 14$ ft   *Write original equation.*
$$d = 14 \div 3.14 \quad \text{\textit{Divide by }} \pi \approx 3.14.$$
$$d \approx 4.46 \text{ in.}$$

2. $C = \pi \cdot d = 9$ m   *Write original equation.*
$$d = 9 \div 3.14 \quad \text{\textit{Divide by }} \pi \approx 3.14.$$
$$d \approx 2.87 \text{ m}$$

Practice and Problem Solving

1. B

2. C

3. A

4. 14.13 ft

5. 7 units

6. 12.56 units

7. 6.28 units

8. 15.7 units

9. 18.84 units

10. 4.71 ft

11. 364.24 mm

12. 32.97 in.

13. 1193.2 mm

14. Perimeter $= 24.8$ in.
Area $= 38.44$ in.^{2}

15. Perimeter $= 21$ m
Area $= 24.5$ m^2

16. 31.4 in.

17. 62.8 in.

18. 25.12 ft

19. 50.24 ft

20. The circumference also doubles.

21. About 191 times

22. 250 ft

23. B

(continued)

24. a. $P = 12.36$ in.

$C =$ About 12.56 in.

b. 12.48 in.

c. Yes; *sample answer:* The greater the number of sides makes the polygon's perimeter closer to the circumference of the circle.

Answers for Lesson 10.6, pages 507–510

Ongoing Assessment

1. 200.96 yd^2

2. 452.16 m^2

3. 19.63 in.^{2}

Practice and Problem Solving

1. A

2. C

3. B

4. D

5. a. 153.86 in.^{2}
   b. 452.16 in.^{2}

6. 176.6 in.^{2}

7. 9.62 ft^2

8. 353 mm^2

9. 11.86 yd^2

10. 175.96 cm^2

11. 200.52 m^2

12. greater than

13. less than

14. greater than

15. 8,342,666 mi^2

16. 10,236.4 mi

17. $\frac{1}{2}$ in.; at a $\frac{1}{2}$-in. setting, the camera has a radius of $\frac{1}{4}$ in. $\frac{1}{4} > \frac{3}{16}$

18. 75.36 cm^2; cylinder

19. C

20. C

21. $\pi \cdot (2r)$, or $2\pi r$

22. Lincoln Memorial: 78,883.87 ft^2
Jefferson Memorial: 315,535.46 ft^2

23. 798 ft

Answers for Spiral Review, page 510

1. Mean: 46.125
   Median: 49
   Mode: 55
   Range: 43

2. Bus: 0.45; walk: 0.275; bike: 0.125; car: 0.15

3. 48°

4. 122°

Answers for Communicating About Mathematics, page 511

1. 20.41 ft

2. Front wheel: 2.75 ft; rear wheels: 5.5 ft

3. The circumference of the back wheel is about twice the circumference of the front wheel.

4. 28.78 yards;

   Circumference of the back wheel: $2 \times \pi \times 5.5 = 34.54$ feet

   Circumference of the front wheel: $\frac{1}{2} \times 34.54 = 17.27$ feet

   Total circumference: $17.27 + 34.54 + 34.54 = 86.25$ feet

   $86.25 \text{ feet} \times \frac{1 \text{ yard}}{3 \text{ feet}} = 28.78$ yards

Answers for Lesson 10.7, pages 513–515

Ongoing Assessment

1. 8; 40°   **2.** 4; 20°   **3.** 3; 15°

Practice and Problem Solving

1. $\frac{1}{12} \neq 40°$; it should be $\frac{1}{12} = 30°$.

2. $\frac{5}{12} \neq 48°$; it should be $\frac{2}{12} = 48°$.

3. D, B, C, A

4. $8\% + 1\% + 10\% + 3\% + 22\% + 56\% = 100\%$;
$\frac{8}{100} + \frac{1}{100} + \frac{10}{100} + \frac{3}{100} + \frac{22}{100} + \frac{56}{100} = 1$

5. Nuclear, oil, and gas; $22 + 10 + 3 = 35$

6. Yes; coal accounts for 56%.

7. $a° = 135°; b° = 120°; c° = 45°; d = \frac{1}{6}$

8. $a° = 60°; b° = 144°; c° = 30°; d = \frac{1}{10}; e = \frac{1}{4}$

9.

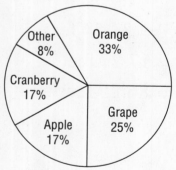

10.

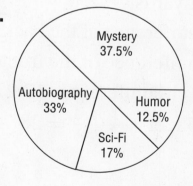

(continued)

11.

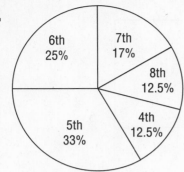

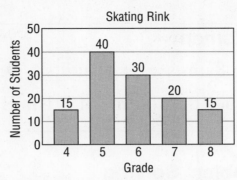

Grades 5 and 7; circle graph ($33\% + 17\% = 50\%$)

12.

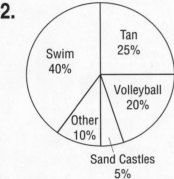

Get a tan: 5; swim: 8; play volleyball: 4; build a sand castle: 1; other: 2

13. A

14. B

15. $18°$; $18°$

Ongoing Assessment

1. A: 4 units^3; B: 8 units^3; C: 12 units^3; D: 16 units^3
2. Prism D has twice the volume of Prism B.

Practice and Problem Solving

1. Length: 6 cm
   Width: 4 cm
   Height: 8 cm

2. No; a cube's length, width, and height are equal; each face is not a square.

3. 208 cm^2

4. 192 cm^3

5. S.A. = 272 m^2
   V = 192 m^3

6. S.A. = 384 in.^{2}
   V = 512 in.^{3}

7. S.A. = 700 ft^2
   V = 1000 ft^3

8. S.A. = 22 in.^{2}
   V = 6 in.^{3}

   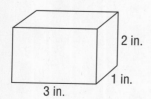

9. S.A. = 96 cm^2
   V = 64 cm^3

10. S.A. = 108 ft^2
    V = 72 ft^3

11. S.A. = 1248 mm^2
    V = 2880 mm^3

12. S.A. = 950 m^2
    V = 1500 m^3

13. S.A. = 364 in.^{2}
    V = 367.5 in.^{3}

14. S.A. = 468 m^2
    V = 648 m^3

15. S.A. = 1800 in.^{2}
    V = 5184 in.^{3}

16. S.A. = 32.58 cm^2
    V = 10.296 cm^3

17. 12 mm

18. 872 ft^2

(continued)

19. 391 ft^2

20. 1632 ft^3

21. 500

22. a. 5184 in.^3 **b.** No

23. C

24. a. $P = 14 \text{ cm}$

$A = 12 \text{ cm}^2$

b. 122 cm^2

c. 122 cm^2

d. You can find the surface area of a prism using the formula

$$\text{Surface area} = Ph + 2B,$$

where P is the perimeter of the prism's base, h is the prism height, and B is the area of the prism's base; yes

1. False

2. True

3. 70°;

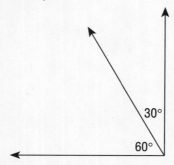

4. 30°;

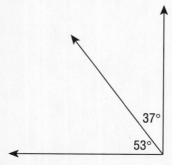

5. 53°;

6. 18°;

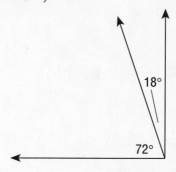

7. *P Q U V*

8. *Q R T V*; *P Q U V*; *P R S V*; *Q R S U*

9. *Q R S U*; *P Q U V*; *P R S V*

10. *P R T V*; *P Q U V*; *P R S V*; *Q R S U*; *Q R S V*; *Q R T U*; *Q R T V*

11. 20 ft^2

12. 12.56 m

13. 16.33 cm

14. 2.36 ft

15. 47.10 in.

16. 314 cm^2

17. 706.50 ft^2

18. 21.23 m^2

19. 50.24 in.^{2}

(continued)

20.

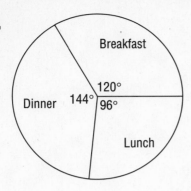

21. S.A. $= 78$ in.^{2}
V $= 45$ in.^{3}

22. S.A. $= 118$ ft^2
V $= 70$ ft^3

23. S.A. $= 72$ m^2
V $= 32$ m^3

1. Intersecting

2. $\overleftrightarrow{ST}$ and $\overleftrightarrow{YZ}$, $\overleftrightarrow{UV}$ and $\overleftrightarrow{YZ}$

3. Supplementary

4. Complementary

5. $\angle 1$ and $\angle 3$ are supplementary, so $\angle 3$ measures $180° - 98° = 82°$; since $\angle 3$ and $\angle 4$ are supplementary and $\angle 3$ measures $82°$, then $\angle 4$ must measure $98°$.

6. Quadrilateral, parallelogram, rectangle; $a = 7$, $b = 4$

7. Quadrilateral, parallelogram, rectangle, square; $a = 9$, $b = 9$

8. Quadrilateral, parallelogram; $a = 3$, $b° = 74°$, $c° = 106°$

9. 54 units^2

10. 48 units^2

11. 52 units^2

12. Circumference $= 43.96$ in.; Area $= 153.86$ in.^{2}

13. Circumference $= 62.8$ cm; Area $= 314$ in.^{2}

14. Circumference $= 9.42$ m; Area $= 7.065$ m^2

15.

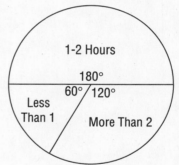

16. 30 in.^{3}; 600 in.^{3}; yes, the volume of the box is the same as the volume of the tapes.

Answers for Standardized Test Practice, page 525

1. D
2. D
3. B
4. C

5. C
6. A
7. C
8. D

Answers for Lesson 11.1, pages 533–535

Ongoing Assessment

1. $-6, -5, -3, 2, 3$; answers vary.
2. $-5, -2, 0, 2, 5$; answers vary.

Practice and Problem Solving

1. $-4, -3, -2, -1, 0, 1, 2, 3, 4$
2. D
3. C
4. E
5. B
6. A
7. -10 is opposite 10;
   8 is opposite -8.
8.
   Increasing by 2; $4, 6$
9.
   Increasing by 2; $5, 7$
10.
   Decreasing by 3; $-10, -13$
11. $>$
12. $>$
13. $<$
14. $<$

15. $>$
16. $>$
17. $<$
18. $<$
19. $-4, -3, 1, 3, 6$
20. $-9, -7, -2, 0, 4$
21. $-6, -5, -3, -1, 0$
22. C
23. B
24. D
25. A
26. 0
27. -5
28. -6
29. 9
30. 1
31. -1
32. -9

(continued)

33. 6

34.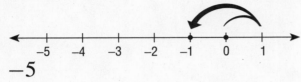

35. $-80°$F in Prospect Creek Camp

36.

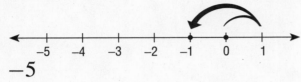

-5

37. C

38. Read across to the Fahrenheit scale; about $18°$F.

Answers for Lesson 11.2, pages 539–541

Ongoing Assessment

1. a. 8 **b.** -6 **c.** -3 **d.** -5
Yes

2. Integer addition is commutative.

Practice and Problem Solving

1. To add five, you need to move right, not left.
$-2 + 5 = 3$

2. To add negative three, you need to move left, not right. $-4 + (-3) = -7$

3. $3 + (-2) = 1$

4. 10

5. -1

6. 4

7. -7

8. If the positive integer lies farther from zero than the negative one, the sum is positive. If the negative integer is farther from zero, the sum is negative. If both integers are the same distance from zero, the sum is zero.

9. $3 + 3 = 6$

10. $0 + (-7) = -7$

11. $-2 + (-7) = -9$

12. $-8 + 4 = -4$

13. A

14. C

15. D

16. B

17. 14

18. 0

(continued)

Answers for Lesson 11.2, pages 539–541 (cont.)

19. -1

20. 3

21. -14

22. -15

23. 7

24. -7

25. $4 + (-5) + 2 = 1$

26. $-3 + (-1) + 5 + (-1) = 0$

27. a. $22 **b.** $11

28. gained 15 yd

29. gained 4 yd

30. D

31. $2°$ C; add temperatures and divide by 7 to get the average.

32. Answers vary.

Answers for Spiral Review, page 542

1. $\frac{4}{15}$

2. $\frac{1}{2}$

3. $\frac{3}{8}$

4. $\frac{1}{4}$

5. True; $\frac{5}{6} = \frac{5 \times 3}{6 \times 3} = \frac{15}{18}$

6. False; $\frac{2}{9} = \frac{2 \times 3}{9 \times 3} = \frac{6}{27} \neq \frac{5}{27}$

7. True; $\frac{15}{45} = \frac{1 \times 15}{3 \times 15} = \frac{1}{3}$

8. False; $\frac{3}{4} = \frac{3 \times 5}{4 \times 5} = \frac{15}{20} \neq \frac{16}{20}$

9. $\frac{9}{8}$

10. 6

11. $\frac{12}{7}$

12. $\frac{16}{13}$

13.

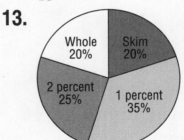

14. $<$

15. $>$

16. $>$

17. $<$

Answers for Lesson 11.3, pages 547–550

Ongoing Assessment

1.
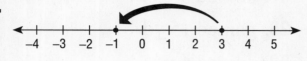
Begin at 3.
Move 4 units to the left.
Final position is −1.

2.
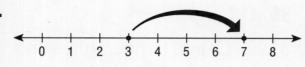
Begin at 3.
Move 4 units to the right.
Final position is 7.

3.
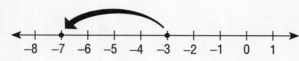
Begin at −3.
Move 4 units to the left.
Final position is −7.

Practice and Problem Solving

1. Left

2. Left

3. Right

4. Right

5. Left, left, right, right; answers remain the same.

6. Answers vary. −35

7. C

8. A

9. D

10. B

11. −10

12. −7

13. 11

14. 8

15. 5

16. −2

17. 52 ft

18. 8 seconds

19. −10

20. 11

21. 2

(continued)

22. 1, 2, 3, 4; with the first number kept the same, as the number being subtracted decreases by 1, the difference increases by 1.

23. 5, 4, 3, 2; with the number being subtracted kept the same, as the first number decreases by 1, the difference decreases by 1.

24. −8, −7, −6, −5; with the first number kept the same, as the number being subtracted decreases by 1, the difference increases by 1.

25. *Sample answer:* Try to box negative numbers, because subtracting a negative number results in addition.

26. A

27. D

28. C

29. D

30. a.

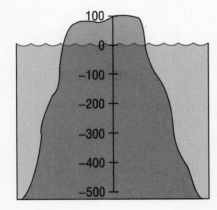

b. 500 below sea level is negative.

$100 - (-500) = 600$ ft

31. 7164 years

Answers for Spiral Review, page 550

1. 7

2. 6

3. 3

4. 3

5. 4

6. 2

7. 3

8. 2

9. Comedy: 116
   Suspense: 40
   Drama: 30
   Westerns: 14

10. $=$

11. $<$

12. $>$

13. $>$

14. $=$

15. $>$

16. $35°$

17. $50°$

18. $125°$

19. $C = 50.24 \text{ m}$
    $A = 200.96 \text{ m}^2$

20. $C = 31.4 \text{ in.}$
    $A = 78.5 \text{ in.}^2$

Answers for Mid-Chapter Assessment, page 551

1. B
2. D
3. C
4. A
5. $<$
6. $>$
7. $<$
8. $>$
9. $>$
10. $<$
11. $<$
12. $>$
13. 2

14. -4
15. -10
16. -6
17. -5
18. -11
19. 11
20. 12
21. $-7 + 4 + (-2) = -5$
22. $-3 + (-5) + 1 = -7$
23. $-4°F; 0°F$
24. $20
25. Answers vary.

Copyright © McDougal Littell Inc. All rights reserved.

Ongoing Assessment

1. $(-4, 7), (-6, 5), (-4, 2), (-5, 5)$

2. $(3, 1), (1, -1), (3, -4), (2, -1)$

Practice and Problem Solving

1. $A(-4, 4), B(4, 3), C(0, 0), D(-3, 1.5), E(-2, -4), F(3, -1)$
   $C(0, 0)$ is called the origin.

2. From $(0, 0)$, move left 3 and up 4.

3. From $(0, 0)$, move right 2 and up 7.

4. From $(0, 0)$, move left 4 and down 6.

5.

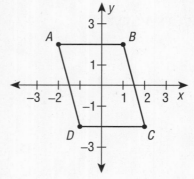

parallelogram

6. Quadrant II

7. Quadrant I

8. Quadrant III

9. Quadrant IV

10.

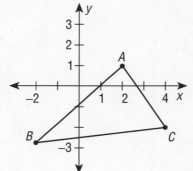

triangle

11.

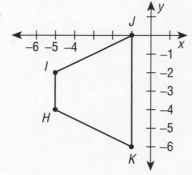

quadrilateral

(continued)

12.

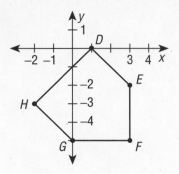

pentagon

13. Original: $(-2, 1), (-1, -1), (-2, -4), (-4, -1)$
New: $(-1, 3), (0, 1), (-1, -2), (-3, 1)$

14. Original: $(1, 2), (2, 4), (4, 4), (3, 1)$
New: $(1, -2), (2, -4), (4, -4), (3, -1)$

15. *Sample answer:* The x-coordinates are opposites.
The y-coordinates are the same.

16.

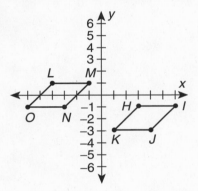

Slide left 7 and up 2

17.

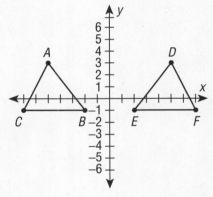

Flip about the y-axis.

18. $(0, 0)$

19. Store #4 is closest; about 15 miles away.

20. #2 and #6; each is 1 unit from the origin along the
x-axis and 4 units from the origin along the y-axis.

(continued)

21. Right 1 unit, down 5 units

22. C

23. **a.** and **b.**

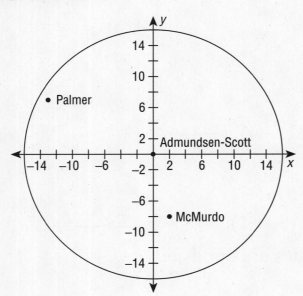

Answers for Lesson 11.5, pages 559–562

Ongoing Assessment

1. $(-3, -5)$, $(-2, -4)$, $(-1, -3)$, $(0, -2)$, $(1, -1)$, $(2, 0)$, $(3, 1)$

2.

3. The points lie on a line; each time x increases by 1, y increases by 1.

Practice and Problem Solving

1. D, C, B, A

2.

x	-2	-1	0	1	2
$x + 3$	1	2	3	4	5
	$(-2, 1)$	$(-1, 2)$	$(0, 3)$	$(1, 4)$	$(2, 5)$

3. The x and y coordinates are the same and the points lie in a line.

4. A, D; because they lie in the line and x and y coordinates are the same.

5.

x	-3	-2	-1	0	1	2	3
$x + 4$	1	2	3	4	5	6	7

As the x-coordinate increases, so does the y-coordinate.

(continued)

6.

x	−3	−2	−1	0	1	2	3
$4 - x$	7	6	5	4	3	2	1

As x-coordinate increases, y-coordinate decreases.

7.

x	Days Late	0	1	2	3	4	5
y	Score	10	8	6	4	2	0

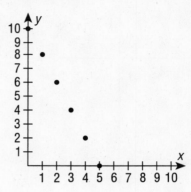

As the x-coordinate increases by 1, the y-coordinate decreases by 2.

8.

x	−3	−2	−1	0	1	2	3
$x - 3$	−6	−5	−4	−3	−2	−1	0

All points lie on a straight line. As x-coordinates increase by 1, y-coordinates increase by 1.

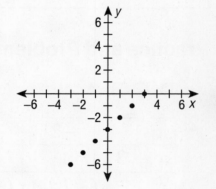

9.

x	−3	−2	−1	0	1	2	3
$-5 + x$	−8	−7	−6	−5	−4	−3	−2

All points lie on a straight line. As x-coordinates increase by 1, y-coordinates increase by 1.

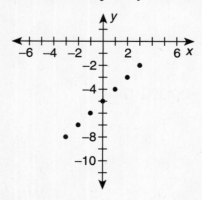

(continued)

10.

x	−3	−2	−1	0	1	2	3
$x - (-4)$	1	2	3	4	5	6	7

All points lie on a straight line. As x-coordinates increase by 1, y-coordinates increase by 1.

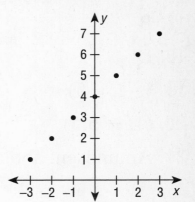

11.

x	−3	−2	−1	0	1	2	3
$x + (-2)$	−5	−4	−3	−2	−1	0	1

All points lie on a straight line. As x-coordinates increase by 1, y-coordinates increase by 1.

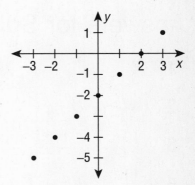

12. C

13. A

14. B

15. *Sample answer:* $(2, -3)$, $(2, 0)$, $(2, 1)$, $(2, 2)$, $(2, 4)$; points should all have the same x-coordinate.

16. a. $(1, -3)$, $(2, -1.5)$, $(3, 0)$, $(4, 1.5)$, $(5, 3)$

b.

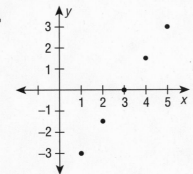

1.5

c. The corn kernel (plant) is 3 inches below the surface of the ground.

(continued)

Answers for Lesson 11.5, pages 559–562 (cont.)

17. B

18. D

19. $(-1, -5)$

20. $(1, -5.5)$

21. Amundsen; about 55 miles

Answers for Spiral Review, pages 562

1. $3\frac{3}{5}$

2. $14\frac{7}{8}$

3. $1\frac{13}{24}$

4. $8\frac{11}{12}$

5. $14\frac{11}{12}$

6. $11\frac{23}{24}$

7. $6\frac{1}{3}$

8. $2\frac{2}{5}$

9. $\frac{1}{3}$

10. $\frac{4}{9}$

11. $\frac{5}{9}$

12. 1

13. $\frac{1}{3}$

14. 3

15. $\frac{1}{15}$

16. $11.25

Ongoing Assessment

1. Answers vary.

2. Answers vary.

3. Yes

Practice and Problem Solving

1. F

2. E

3. A

4. B

5. D

6. C

7. 12 units^2

8. 12.56 units^2

9. 10 units^2

10.

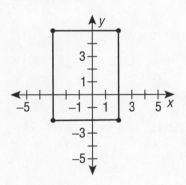

35 units^2

11.

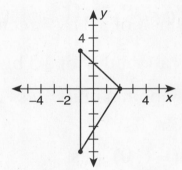

12 units^2

12.

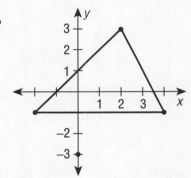

12 units^2

(continued)

Answers for Lesson 11.6, pages 565–567 (cont.)

13.

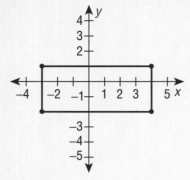

21 units^2

14. B; area is half of a 3 by 4 rectangle.

15. A; area is about that of a 3 by 4 rectangle.

16. B; area is about 4 units^2 less than that of a 4 by 4 square.

17. $(-1, 0), (-1, 0)$; yes

18. $(0, 1), (0, 0)$; no

19. $(0, 0), (0, 0)$; yes

20.
Triangle	Area
ABC	16 units^2
DEF	4 units^2
GHI	1 unit^2
JKL	$\frac{1}{4}$ unit^2

Area of each triangle is $\frac{1}{4}$ of the area of the next larger triangle. The area of the next smaller triangle would be $\frac{1}{16}$ unit^2.

21. 12 units^2; 48 mi^2

22. D

23. A

24. Answers vary.

Answers for Chapter Review, pages 569–571

1.

$-6, -5, -2, 0, 2, 5$

2. 5

3. -14

4. $-1°C$

5. 9

6. 0

7. -5

8. 3 points

9. 4

10. 6

11. -2

12. -11

13. 0

14. 3

15. 17

16. -3

17. $(-4, 0)$

18. $(2, 2)$

19. $(-1, -3)$

20. $(4, -3)$

21. Quadrant III

22.–29.

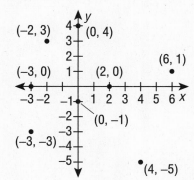

30.

x	-2	-1	0	1	2
$4 - x$	6	5	4	3	2

The points lie in a decreasing line.

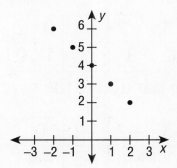

31. $(0, -3), (2, 0), (-2, 0)$

32. 24 units^2

33. $(-8, 2), (3, 2)$; about 220 mi

Answers for Chapter Assessment, page 572

1. −8

2. −3

3. −7

4. 6

5. 0

6. 16

7. 5

8. −30

9. −8

10. −5

11. 4

12.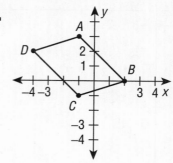

parallelogram

13.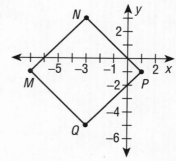

square

14.

x	−3	−2	−1	0	1	2	3
$1 - x$	4	3	2	1	0	−1	−2

This line is parallel to the given line.

15.

x	−3	−2	−1	0	1	2	3
$x - 4$	−7	−6	−5	−4	−3	−2	−1

This line is perpendicular to the given line.

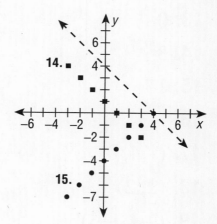

16. 15 units^2

17. 15 units^2

18. 12.56 units^2

19. B; answers vary.

20. Answers vary.

Answers for Standardized Test Practice, page 573

1. D
2. C
3. C
4. B
5. A

6. A
7. A
8. C
9. B
10. B

Answers for Lesson 12.1, pages 581–583

Practice and Problem Solving

1. Write the original equation. Subtract 2 from each side. Solution: x is by itself.

2. Write the original equation. Subtract 1 from each side. Solution: m is by itself.

3. Write the original equation. Subtract 3 from each side. Solution: t is by itself.

4. Write the original equation. Subtract the same number from each side. Solution: variable is by itself. Check the solution.

5. -1

6. 3

7. -8

8. $n + 5 = -10; -15$

9. Yes

10. Yes

11. Yes

12. No; $m = -6$

13. -5

14. -8

15. 8

16. 4

17. 0

18. -9

19. 20

(continued)

20. 13

21. 10

22. 203

23. 216

24. 1

25. $x + 2 = 210; 208$

26. $x + 16 = 1; -15$

27. $5 + x = 18; 13$

28. $13 + x = 0; -13$

29. $9 + x = -5; -14$

30. -4

31. $-3 + 2 = -1$

32. $1 = -2 + 3$

33. Labels: Amount saved $= \$38$
Amount left to save $= x$
Cost $= \$64$
Equation: $38 + x = 64$
$x = 26$; you need to save \$26.

34. A; *Sample answer:* B has the bowling ball cost as -48, which is impossible.

35. C

36. Yes, the amount you need to reach 100 point is the amount a in the equation $79 + a = 100; a = 21$. To score 21 points, roll all 4 dot-side up 2 times. On your third roll, only the piece with 1 dot lands dot-side up. On your fourth roll, the remaining 3 pieces land dot-side down.

Answers for Lesson 12.2, pages 585–587

Ongoing Assessment

1.–3. Add the number so that the variable is isolated.

1. 12   **2.** 1   **3.** 9

Practice and Problem Solving

1. Add 3 to both sides of the equation in order to isolate the variable; $t = 17$.

2. Subtract 5 from both sides of the equation in order to isolate the variable; $u = -38$.

3. Add 12 to both sides of the equation in order to isolate the variable; $s = -2$.

4. Original temperature − Change = New temperature

5. Original Temperature = x, Change = 5, New temperature = 28; $x - 5 = 28$

6. $x = 33$; the temperature at 5 P.M. was $33°$ F.

7. Add 8 to each side instead of -8.

$$x - 8 = 7$$
$$x - 8 + 8 = 7 + 8$$
$$x = 15$$

8. Add -6 to each side instead of subtracting -6.

$$x - (-6) = -5$$
$$x - (-6) + (-6) = -5 + -6$$
$$x = -11$$

(continued)

Answers for Lesson 12.2, pages 585–587 (cont.)

9.–11. Answers vary.

12. Yes

13. Yes

14. No; 8

15. No; 2

16. No; −7

17. Yes

18. 21

19. 26

20. 40

21. 65

22. 12

23. 4

24. 15

25. −3

26. −14

27. Labels: Distance in July (million mi) $= x$

Distance in January (million mi) $= 91$

Equation: $x - 3 = 91$

Earth is about 94 million mi from the sun in July.

28. Verbal model: Distance left $=$ Total distance $-$ Distance driven

Labels: Distance left (mi) $= 15$

Total distance (mi) $= x$

Distance driven (mi) $= 35$

Equation: $15 = x - 35$

$x = 50$

The total distance to the museum is 50 mi.

29. C

30. C

31. Total spaces $-$ Open spaces $=$ Playing pieces;

$s - 11 = 14; s = 25$

Answers for Spiral Review, pages 588

1. 3

2. 20

3. 3.3

4. 1.8

5. $\frac{3}{4}$

6. $\frac{5}{7}$

7.

-7	$\xrightarrow{+8}$	1	$\xrightarrow{-4}$	-3	$\xrightarrow{-1}$	-4	$\xrightarrow{+7}$	3

8.

0	$\xrightarrow{+5}$	5	$\xrightarrow{-3}$	2	$\xrightarrow{-6}$	-4	$\xrightarrow{-2}$	-6

9. Ratio; answers vary.

10. Rate; answers vary.

11. Ratio; answers vary.

Answers for Lesson 12.3, pages 591–594

Ongoing Assessment

1.
$$
\begin{aligned}
m + 4.3 &= 3.7 \quad &&\text{Write equation.}\\
-4.3 \quad &-4.3 \quad &&\text{Subtract 4.3 from each side.}\\
\hline
m &= -0.6 \quad &&\text{Solution: } m \text{ is by itself.}
\end{aligned}
$$

2.
$$
\begin{aligned}
y - 3\tfrac{1}{2} &= 2\tfrac{1}{4} \quad &&\text{Write equation.}\\
+3\tfrac{1}{2} \quad &+3\tfrac{1}{2} \quad &&\text{Add } 3\tfrac{1}{2} \text{ to each side.}\\
\hline
y &= 5\tfrac{3}{4} \quad &&\text{Solution: } y \text{ is by itself.}
\end{aligned}
$$

3.
$$
\begin{aligned}
5.1 + x &= 2.5 \quad &&\text{Write equation.}\\
-5.1 \quad &-5.1 \quad &&\text{Subtract 5.1 from each side.}\\
\hline
&x = -2.6 \quad &&\text{Solution: } x \text{ is by itself.}
\end{aligned}
$$

Practice and Problem Solving

1. Subtract $\frac{1}{6}$ from each side.

2. Subtract 7.6 from each side.

3. Add 9.4 to each side.

4. $x - \frac{1}{2} = \frac{2}{3}$

5. $1\frac{3}{8}$

6. $\frac{1}{10}$

7. 15.7

8. $24.91 = 23.50 + t$; \$1.41

9. D

10. C

11. A

12. B

13. Subtract 4.6 from both sides of the equation.
$$
\begin{aligned}
x + 4.6 &= 7.8\\
-4.6 &= -4.6\\
\hline
x &= 3.2
\end{aligned}
$$

14. Add 5.6 to both sides of the equation.
$$
\begin{aligned}
n - 5.6 &= 8.8\\
+5.6 &= +5.6\\
\hline
n &= 14.4
\end{aligned}
$$

15. $\frac{4}{7}$

16. $\frac{6}{8}$, or $\frac{3}{4}$

17. 6.05

(continued)

Answers for Lesson 12.3, pages 591–594 (cont.)

18. $1\frac{5}{12}$

19. 31.39

20. 40.00

21. $\frac{6}{7}$

22. $\frac{4}{9}$

23. -8.6

24. $\frac{1}{2}$

25. 7.78

26. 10.1

27. $\frac{1}{7}, \frac{2}{7}, \frac{3}{7}$; t increases by $\frac{1}{7}$; $\frac{4}{7}$, and $\frac{5}{7}$.

28. 10.25, 15.25, 20.25; t increases by 5; 25.25, 30.25.

29. 36.9, 36.8, 36.7; t decreases by 0.1; 36.6, 36.5.

30. a or d; each shows a true equation of the verbal model.

31. $x + 0.4 = 1$, 0.6 or $x + \frac{2}{5} = 1$, $\frac{3}{5}$

32. Distance to go + Distance walked = Total distance
Distance to go $= x$, Distance walked $= 2.4$,
Total distance $= 4.25$, $x + 2.4 = 4.25$; $x = 1.85$

33. C

34. D

35. B

36.

15.8	1.1	11.6
5.3	9.5	13.7
7.4	17.9	3.2

$\frac{4}{5}$	$\frac{1}{10}$	$\frac{3}{5}$
$\frac{3}{10}$	$\frac{1}{2}$	$\frac{7}{10}$
$\frac{2}{5}$	$\frac{9}{10}$	$\frac{1}{5}$

To complete a square, first find the sum of the complete diagonal or column. Then write an equation in which the unknown square is x. The sum of x and the two known squares in the diagonal, row, or column should be set equal to the sum of a complete diagonal, row, or column. Then solve for x.

37. $x + \frac{1}{3} = 1$; $x = \frac{2}{3}$

Answers for Spiral Review, page 594

1. 6%

2. 5.2

3.

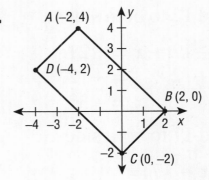

4. about $5.27

5. about $1.40

6. about $9.74

7. 5

8. 7

9. 3

10. 2

11.

Quadrilateral,
parallelogram, rectangle

Answers for Mid-Chapter Assessment, page 595

1. Subtract; 6

2. Add; 29

3. Subtract; −19

4. Add; 5

5. Add 12 to both sides.

$$\begin{aligned} -12 + x &= \ \ \ 21 \\ +12 \ \ \ \ \ \ &= +12 \\ \hline x &= \ \ \ 33 \end{aligned}$$

6. Add 17 to both sides.

$$\begin{aligned} x - 17 &= \ \ \ 16 \\ +17 &= +17 \\ \hline x \ \ \ \ \ \ &= \ \ \ 33 \end{aligned}$$

7. Subtract 5 from both sides.

$$\begin{aligned} -2 &= x + 5 \\ -5 &= \ \ \ -5 \\ \hline -7 &= x \end{aligned}$$

8. −17

9. 41

10. 21

11. −16

12. $\frac{46}{9}$

13. 3.44

14. $\frac{23}{24}$

15. 31.35

16. A; $55.25

17. A; $2\frac{5}{8}$ in.

18. Labels: Total needed ($) $= t$

Amount raised ($) $= 284$

Amount left to raise ($) $= 416$

Equation: $t - 284 = 416$

$$t = 700$$

The class needs to raise $700.

Answers for Lesson 12.4, pages 597–599

Ongoing Assessment

1.

Input, x	Output, y
−2	4
−1	3
0	2
1	1
2	0

2. $(-2, 4), (-1, 3), (0, 2), (1, 1), (2, 0)$

3.

The points lie in a line.

Practice and Problem Solving

1.

Input, x	Output, y
9	1
8	0
7	−1
6	−2
5	−3

2.

Month	Number, m	Temp., T
Jan.	1	4
Feb.	2	8
March	3	12
April	4	16
May	5	20
June	6	24

(continued)

Answers for Lesson 12.4, pages 597–599 (cont.)

3.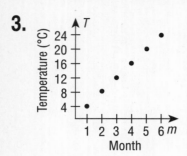

4. No; this function would make temperatures in December higher than temperatures in July.

5. Let e = eggs and let c = number of cartons.
$e = 12 \times c$

6.

Input, x	Output, y
−1	−2
0	−1
1	0
2	1
3	2

$y = x - 1$

7.

Input, m	Output, y
0	0
1	5
2	10
3	15

8.

Input, m	Output, y
0	10
1	11
2	12
3	13

9.

Input, m	Output, y
0	−4
1	−3
2	−2
3	−1

10.

Input, m	Output, y
0	−1
1	0
2	1
3	2

11.

Input, m	Output, y
0	0
1	3
2	6
3	9

12.

Input, m	Output, y
0	8
1	7
2	6
3	5

13.

Input, m	Output, y
0	7
1	8
2	9
3	10

(continued)

Passport to Mathematics Book 1

14.

Input, m	Output, y
0	−2
1	1
2	4
3	7

15. $y = 3x$

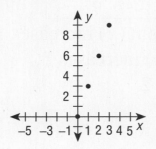

16. $y = x - 6$

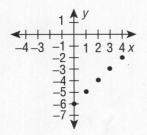

17. $y = x + 5$

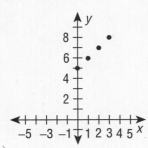

18.

Input, l	Output, C
2	21.5
4	43
6	64.5
8	86

$C = 10.75x$

19.

Input, x	Output, y
0	−2
1	−1
2	0
3	1

B

20.

Input, x	Output, y
−2	0
−1	1
0	2
1	3

C

21.

Input, x	Output, y
−2	−2
−1	−1
0	0
1	1
2	2

A

(continued)

22.

Input, x	Output, y
1	5
2	10
3	15
4	20
5	25
6	30

When input (x) increases 1, output (y) increases 5; $y = \frac{1}{2} \cdot 10 \cdot x$, or $y = 5x$.

23.

Input, x	Output, y
1	3
2	6
3	9
4	12
5	15
6	18

When input (x) increases 1, output (y) increases 3; $y = 3x$

24.

Input, x	Output, y
1	3
2	4
3	5
4	6
5	7
6	8

When input (x) increases 1, output (y) increases 1; $y = x + 2$

25. A

26. Answers vary.

Answers for Lesson 12.5, pages 603–606

Ongoing Assessment

1.

G1, S1, T1	G1, S2, T1	G1, S3, T1
G1, S1, T2	G1, S2, T2	G1, S3, T2
G1, S1, T3	G1, S2, T3	G1, S3, T3
G1, S1, T4	G1, S2, T4	G1, S3, T4
G1, S1, T5	G1, S2, T5	G1, S3, T5
G2, S1, T1	G2, S2, T1	G2, S3, T1
G2, S1, T2	G2, S2, T2	G2, S3, T2
G2, S1, T3	G2, S2, T3	G2, S3, T3
G2, S1, T4	G2, S2, T4	G2, S3, T4
G2, S1, T5	G2, S2, T5	G2, S3, T5

2. *Sample answer:* The counting principle is quicker, especially if there are many choices.

Practice and Problem Solving

1. 6 choices

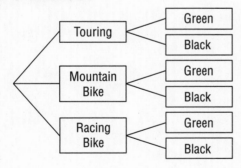

2. 676

3. *Sample answer:* counting principle; 100,000

4. *Sample answer:* either tree diagram or counting principle; 8

5. *Sample answer:* counting principle; 90

6. *Sample answer:* combinations of two skirts and three blouses

7. 9

8. 6

9. $\frac{1}{64}$

10. 10

11. $\frac{1}{18}$

12. 120

13. No; there are exactly 60 combinations.

(continued)

Answers for Lesson 12.5, pages 603–606 (cont.)

14. 144

15. a. 45 **b.** $\frac{1}{15}$

16. D

17. C

18.

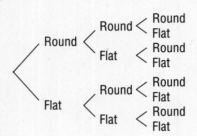

There are 8 ways for the cane dice to land.

19. a. 120

b. No; once a performer performs, he/she will not perform again. That is, there are only 4 possible performers available for the second performance.

c. Answers vary.

Answers for Spiral Review, page 606

1. $\frac{1}{2}$

2. $\frac{9}{10}$

3. $\frac{41}{100}$

4. $\frac{3}{4}$

5. $120°$

6. $51°$

7. $47°$

8. Number increases by $\frac{1}{8}$; $\frac{5}{8}$, $\frac{3}{4}$, $\frac{7}{8}$

9. Number decreases by 3; -7, -10, -13

10. Blue: $\frac{5}{18}$, red $\frac{4}{9}$, green $\frac{1}{6}$, and yellow $\frac{1}{9}$

Answers for Communicating About Mathematics, page 607

1. *Sample answer:* A random event would be when an object moves or is thrown in front of your character's path. The game acts as a function machine when you press a button to make your character jump or when you press a button to make a race car turn.

2. **a.** $P = x + 10$

   b. $S = z - 2$

3. *Sample answer:* For part (a) you input the number of points x the player has before hitting a circle and the output P is the number of points the player has after hitting a circle. For part (b) you input the number of points z the player has before hitting a square and the output S is the number of points the player has after hitting a square.

4. *Sample answer:* Ask each student in the class if they have a video game system at home. You expect $\frac{1}{3}$ of the class to have a video game system at home.

Answers for Lesson 12.6, pages 609–611

Ongoing Assessment

1. $\frac{9}{30}$, or $\frac{3}{10}$ **2.** $\frac{9}{30}$, or $\frac{3}{10}$ **3.** Answers vary.

Practice and Problem Solving

1. Occurrence of one event doesn't affect the other event. You can find the probability by (1) using the product of their probabilities or (2) by making a list.

2. Yes; playing video games isn't affected by liking to swim.

3. No; the fact that it is raining does affect the use of an umbrella.

4. GG_1, GG_2, GB, GY, GR, BG_1, BG_2, BB, BY, BR, YG_1, YG_2, YB, YY, YR, RG_1, RG_2, RB, RY, RR; since 2 of the 20 possibilities are both green, the probability is $\frac{1}{10}$.

5. a. Answers vary.
   b. Estimate: $\frac{1}{45}$
   c. Theoretical: $\frac{1}{45}$

6. No; studying affects the outcome of a test.

7. Yes; owning a dog has no effect on liking to roller skate.

8. No; playing baseball affects whether you need cleats.

9. $\frac{2}{5}$ **11.** $\frac{5}{8}$ **13.** B

10. $\frac{8}{99}$ **12.** $\frac{1}{8}$ **14. a.** $\frac{14,641}{160,000}$

b. $\frac{6561}{160,000}$; answers vary.

Answers for Chapter Review, pages 613 and 614

1. -15
2. -2
3. -2
4. 3
5. -2
6. -10
7. -20
8. -7
9. -5
10. 3
11. -1
12. -4
13. 20
14. 14
15. 16
16. -1
17. $3\frac{1}{2} + x = 8; 4\frac{1}{2}$ mi
18. $x - 12.25 = 3.50; \$15.75$

19.

Input, x	Output, y
-1	-4
0	-3
1	-2
2	-1
3	0

20.

Input, x	Output, y
-1	4
0	5
1	6
2	7
3	8

21.

Input, x	Output, y
-1	2
0	3
1	4
2	5
3	6

22.

Input, x	Output, y
-1	-7
0	-6
1	-5
2	-4
3	-3

23. 9 figures
24. $\frac{1}{8}$
25. **a.** No; practicing tennis every day can affect whether you are chosen for the tennis team.

   b. Yes; taking a quiz in math class has no effect on the sun shining.

Answers for Chapter Assessment, page 615

1. -7

2. -25

3. $\frac{8}{11}$

4. 9.23

5. -40

6. $1\frac{7}{15}$

7. 18.03

8. -1

9. 18

10.

Input, x	Output, y
-3	0
-2	1
-1	2
0	3
1	4

$y = x + 3$

11.

Input, x	Output, y
-4	-5
-3	-4
-2	-3
-1	-2
0	-1

$y = x - 1$

12.

Input, x	Output, y
0	1
1	2
2	3
3	4
4	5

$y = x + 1$

13. Score before Round 2 − Points lost in Round 2 = Score after Round 2

$$s - 55 = -15$$
$$s = 40$$

14. Initial number of plants − Plants planted = Remaining plants

$$p - 11 = 13$$
$$p = 24$$

15. 192

16. $\frac{1}{64}$

17. $\frac{1}{4}$

18. $\frac{1}{128}$

Answers for Standardized Test Practice, page 616

1. A
2. A
3. A
4. A

5. D
6. D
7. B
8. C

Answers for Cumulative Review, pages 617 and 618

1. $8\frac{1}{5}$
2. $8\frac{7}{16}$
3. $2\frac{1}{3}$
4. $4\frac{15}{16}$
5. D; $\frac{5}{12}$
6. A; $\frac{1}{7}$
7. B; $\frac{2}{5}$
8. C; $\frac{9}{32}$
9. $2\frac{4}{7}$
10. $2\frac{3}{4}$
11. $a = 4\,\text{ft}$ $e = 110°$
    $b = 70°$ $f = 3.7\,\text{ft}$
    $c = 5\,\text{ft}$ $g = 90°$
    $d = 90°$ $h = 3.8\,\text{ft}$
12. $a = 12\,\text{cm}$ $e = 105°$
    $b = 105°$ $f = 12\,\text{cm}$
    $c = 17\,\text{cm}$ $g = 90°$
    $d = 60°$ $h = 17\,\text{cm}$

13. Right, scalene
14. Equilateral, isosceles, acute
15. Acute, scalene
16. Right, isosceles
17. 7
18. -13
19. 0
20. -15
21. 7
22. -7
23. $12.56\,\text{units}^2$
24. $10\,\text{units}^2$
25. $16\,\text{units}^2$
26. 11 ft; answers vary.
27. $x + 3.36 = 59.36$; $56.00
28. 26
29. 15

(continued)

Answers for Cumulative Review, pages 617 and 618 (cont.)

30. 16

31. $\frac{7}{8}$

32. 14.72

33. 40.72

34. 6

35. 9

36. $\frac{1}{4}$

37. Answers vary.